word 2000
made
painless

THIS IS A CARLTON BOOK

Text and design copyright © Carlton Books 2000

A CIP Catalogue for this book is available from the British Library

ISBN 1 85868 935 X

Project Editor: Lara Maiklem
Production: Sarah Corteel

Created by Gecko Grafx Ltd

Notice of Liability
Every effort has been made to ensure that this book contains accurate and
current information. However, the Publisher and the author shall not be
liable for any loss or damage suffered by the readers as a result of any
information contained herein.

Trademarks
Microsoft®, Microsoft Word 2000®, Microsoft Office 2000® and
Windows® are registered trademarks of Microsoft Corporation.
All other trademarks are acknowledged as belonging to their respective
companies

Printed and bound in Italy

word 2000 made painless

Christophe Dillinger

CARLTON
BOOKS

CONTENTS

GETTING STARTED

1

Microsoft Word is probably the best known word processor available, and has been so for a long time. Part of the Office 2000 package, the latest version – Word 2000 – is a large program that can seem intimidating at first. Do not worry though: the people at Microsoft know their business and have made sure that it is clear, intuitive and easy to use. Intelligent functions and personalized menus make working a creative experience. Whatever your word processing needs, business, personal or creative, intelligent tools and help functions are only a few clicks or buttons away.

INSTALLING WORD 2000

Installing Word from Office 2000 is just a matter of putting the CD into the drive and answering a few questions. You will be presented with a screen asking you some personal details such as your name, initials and the long CD key (the product's serial number). Punch all this in and click on <u>Next</u>. The CD key is not case sensitive, which means that you can type it in lower or upper case and it will still work.

1 Enter your "customer information" and CD Key in the opening installation screen.

The plain box on the left-hand side tells you where you are in the installation process.

Welcome to Microsoft Office 2000

Welcome to Microsoft Office 2000

This is the Installation Wizard for Microsoft Office 2000 Premium. It will guide you through the installation process.

SETUP

Customer Information

License and Support Information

Ready to Install

Installing Office

Please enter your customer information:

<u>U</u>ser name

<u>I</u>nitials

O<u>r</u>ganization

In the boxes below, type your 25-character CD Key. You'll find this number on the yellow sticker on the back of the CD jewel case.

CD Key:

[____]-[____]-[____]-[____]-[____]

Help | Cancel | << <u>B</u>ack | <u>N</u>ext >>

BACK

Forgotten something or made a mistake along the way? Click Back anytime and you will be taken to the previous window. Once you are sure of your choice or when all the necessary information has been entered, the Next button will become active. Click it to proceed to the next stage. Confused? Click the Help button anytime. And if you started installing Office 2000 but you have to leave for an emergency meeting, hit Cancel and come back to it later. The next stage will be agreeing to the standard Microsoft licence. Then you will be taken to the installation options screen. For most people, just clicking on the Install Now box will be the best way of getting everything installed. However, if you do want to change the Office's default settings, you'll need to Customize it.

Install Now will do just that: copy and set up all the files needed to install the full Microsoft Office 2000 on your hard drive. This gives you a minimum of fuss.

The Customize... button will let you specify which programs you want to install and where you want to install them, as well as the options you wish to use. This is for advanced users or people who have worked with previous versions of Word already.

Setup is ready to install Microsoft Office 2000 Premiu

Click Install Now to begin installing Office...

Install Now
Install Office 2000 at c:\Program Files\Microsoft Offi

...or click Customize to make more choices about your Office inst

Customize...
Choose the installation location, indicate whether or
previous versions of Office, and specify which featu

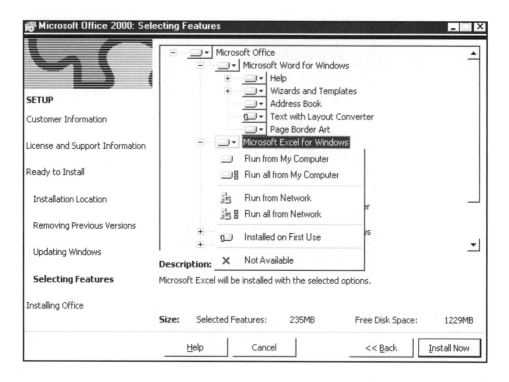

CUSTOM INSTALLATION

There are two main tasks involved in performing a custom installation of the Microsoft Office. One is to choose a location on your hard drive for the programs to be installed into, and the other is selecting which Office components are going to be included. Selecting a location is relatively simple. You can either accept the default option of installing the Office into the newly-created <u>Microsoft Office</u> subdirectory of the <u>C:/Program Files/</u> directory, or you can browse to, or type, a new location for the install to take place in.

Choosing which parts of the Office to install – known as <u>Selecting Features</u> – is quite a lot more complicated, as the picture above shows. The contents of the Microsoft Office are displayed in the Microsoft Office 2000: Selecting Features dialog. At first, this will show you a list of the main components of the Office – Word, Excel, Outlook and so on – available with the version you have purchased. The programs are shown as a file map, with a + sign before them to indicate that some components of that program are still hidden. You can click on the + to reveal the next layer of extra programs associated with that program. For example, <u>Microsoft Word for Windows</u> hides the <u>Help</u> components, which in turn hides the <u>Office Assistant</u> components, and so on. Clicking on the drop-down box just to the left of each item lets you choose to install it (<u>Run From My Computer</u>), install it and all its components (<u>Run All From My Computer</u>), install it when you first start it (<u>Installed on First Use</u>), or not install it at all (<u>Not Available</u>). The icon for that component will change as appropriate. If the icon is white, that component and all its subcomponents are due to be installed either immediately or on first use. If there is no + for the item, it has no sub-components. If you want a full installation of Word, click on it and select <u>Run All From My Computer</u>. So long as the <u>Selected Features</u> total is less than the <u>Free Disk Space</u> total, the installation will fit on your hard drive. When you have selected the various components you want, click on the <u>Install Now</u> button and your custom installation will be performed. You can add or remove bits later by running the Office 2000 CD again, so it doesn't matter too much if you miss something, or install more than you wanted.

RUNNING WORD

The Installation process will place icons for the Microsoft Office programs that you install into your Programs folder for you automatically. These are shown above, and provide a handy short-cut for starting Word or any other component of the Microsoft Office.

FILE MANAGEMENT

Being organized is a very important part of productive working. Making sure that you have all the components you need to store and retrieve your documents, and establishing a clear, easy-to-use file system are essential starting points for productive use of Word 2000. So, let's start Word 2000 and get going.

In order to make sure that you can find your work when you need it, use Windows Explorer to create a folder on your computer where you will store all your work. By default, you can use the My Documents folder. It is often useful to subdivide your folder into one or more layers of subfolders, each one having a sensible, easy to remember name – such as Personal or Letters, or by clients' names. If you already use such a file system at the office, try to duplicate it on your computer – if you know it works, use it!

This is what Word 2000 looks like when you start. It opens in <u>Print View</u> mode by default, with an empty document open and ready to use.

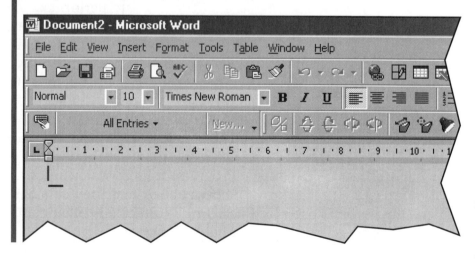

At the top of your work window are a menu bar and row of icons. Each icon is in fact a short cut to a command in the menu bar. You can customize the way they all look, and we'll show you how to do that later. Word 2000 will also customize itself for you automatically, by remembering the functions you use most. You can use either the icons or the menu bar to access the various functions available in Word 2000.

Click on the <u>New</u> icon to start a new document.

Click the <u>Open</u> icon to load an existing file.

Click the <u>Save</u> icon to save your current work.

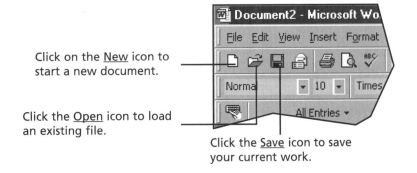

The file menu can be used to open, create and save documents. Check out the keyboard shortcuts: hit <u>Ctrl+N</u> for a new document, <u>Ctrl+O</u> to open a document you have already saved, and <u>Ctrl+S</u> to quickly save your work to disk.

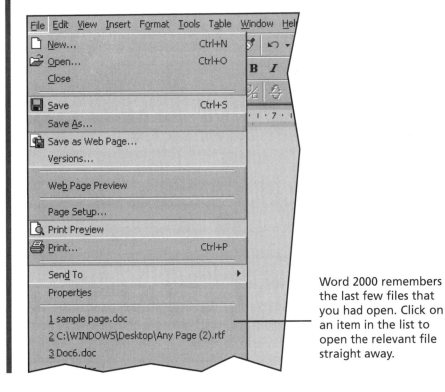

Word 2000 remembers the last few files that you had open. Click on an item in the list to open the relevant file straight away.

THE OPEN DIALOG BOX

When you select <u>Open</u> to load a previously-saved document, you'll see the <u>Open</u> dialog box. You can use this window to navigate around your files as you would in Windows Explorer.

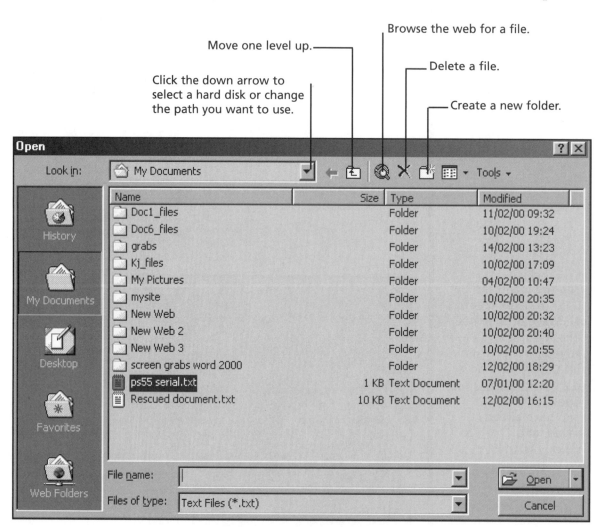

Browse the web for a file.

Move one level up.

Delete a file.

Click the down arrow to select a hard disk or change the path you want to use.

Create a new folder.

Word will open many different file types in several different formats. Clicking on the down arrow to the right of the <u>Files of type</u> box will show a list of file types that Word 2000 can open. To add to this list, see page 11. The default setting is "Word documents" and will show you all the files that the program recognizes as being documents that were created by Word 2000. If you keep documents in a variety of formats, you can select one particular type and the file list box will show only the files matching that type. This is very handy if you work with different file formats or older documents. When saving, you can select an item from the same list to distribute your work to Macintosh systems, older versions of Word, or even files created with other programs, such as Lotus 1-2-3.

The "Look in" panel, to the left of the Open dialog box, enables you to quickly move to one of Windows' special folders.

Browse through your recently accessed files.

"My Documents" is Windows' default document storage folder.

Select from files saved on your desktop.

For the files you put in the Favorites folder.

Use this icon to browse your files stored over the web.

MANY BEGINNINGS   ▭▢✕

There is more than one way to launch Word 2000. You can select the Start button from the menu bar, then choose Programs and then Word. You can also right-click anywhere on the desktop and choose Word Document from the New submenu. You can also double-click on an existing Word 2000 document, and the program will start and open the file automatically. Each document will open in its own separate window.

S TARTING A DOCUMENT

Starting a new document is as simple as knowing what you want to do and then doing it. Create a new document using <u>FILE/NEW</u> in the menu bar.

When you select <u>New</u> from the <u>File</u> menu bar, the template window opens. If you type the shortcut <u>Ctrl+N</u> or click the <u>New Document</u> icon, the default template (the <u>Normal</u> or <u>Blank Document</u> template) will automatically be used. You can use, create and modify other templates as you wish. A template is a pre-prepared document that contains all the headings, layout and other formatting appropriate for a particular type of document, such as a letter or web page.

Select the way the templates are displayed: Choose between <u>Large icons</u>, <u>List</u> and <u>Detail</u> view.

When a template is fully installed, you can get a preview by just clicking on it.

Use the tabs to select the type of document you want to create.

Choose the template that best matches the type of document you want to create. If you do not have that template already installed, Word 2000 will ask you to insert your installation CD-ROM and will install it for you.

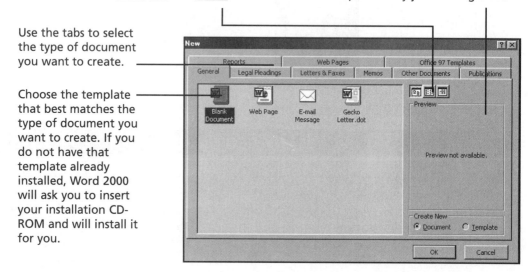

CLICK AND TYPE

If you do not wish to use a pre-prepared template, select the General tab and pick Blank Document. This is the default setting for Word, and the one you will most often use.

With the new "click and type" feature, you can type on the left ...in the middle... on the right... anywhere!

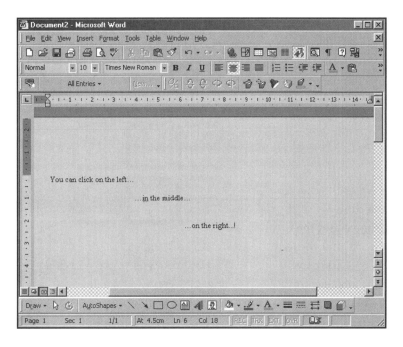

Thanks to an impressive new feature, you can now double-click anywhere on the page and start typing. If you make a mistake, use the mouse to position the cursor where the mistake is. Using the Delete key will erase the character straight after the cursor, while Backspace will erase the character just before the cursor. The mouse is the easiest way to navigate around a document: move it to where you want to be – or the item to select – and click. You can use keyboard commands without moving the mouse, of course.

INSERTING AND OVERWRITING

You can toggle between Overwrite and Insert mode by hitting the Insert key. Overwrite will put the text you type over any letters that were already there, while Insert will move existing text along the line to make room for your new typing.

Overwrite mode, as shown in the info bar.

IMPORTANT KEYS

When using an extended keyboard, the following keys will prove to be essential very quickly:

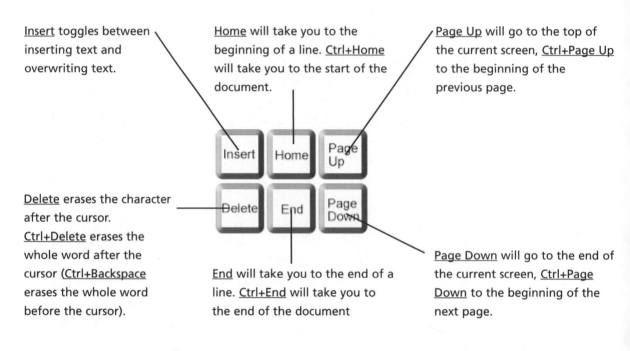

Insert toggles between inserting text and overwriting text.

Home will take you to the beginning of a line. Ctrl+Home will take you to the start of the document.

Page Up will go to the top of the current screen, Ctrl+Page Up to the beginning of the previous page.

Delete erases the character after the cursor. Ctrl+Delete erases the whole word after the cursor (Ctrl+Backspace erases the whole word before the cursor).

End will take you to the end of a line. Ctrl+End will take you to the end of the document

Page Down will go to the end of the current screen, Ctrl+Page Down to the beginning of the next page.

Navigating your document is usually much faster using the keyboard shortcuts than it is using the mouse.

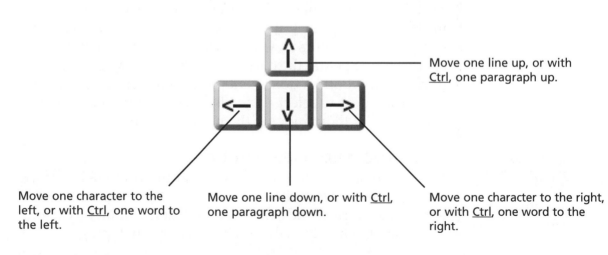

Move one line up, or with Ctrl, one paragraph up.

Move one character to the left, or with Ctrl, one word to the left.

Move one line down, or with Ctrl, one paragraph down.

Move one character to the right, or with Ctrl, one word to the right.

WORD'S TEMPLATES

By selecting <u>NEW</u> from the <u>FILE</u> menu, you can select a new template to base your work on. Pick one of the templates that is already installed, such as the "Contemporary Letter" in the Letters and Faxes Tab (shown below) to get an idea of the kinds of material available.

Some elements can be moved around or stretched. If you click on an element and a "bounding box" appears (top right on this illustration), you can use the eight handle points to resize it, or click on the box and drag to move it.

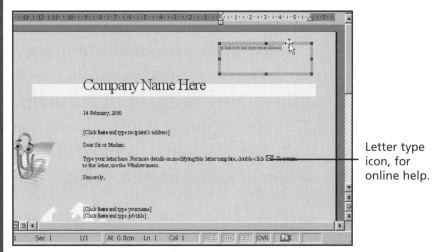

Letter type icon, for online help.

The Template is a collection of elements you can modify at will. Just click where you are asked to enter some text (ie Company Name Here) and type. You can change the font, the colours, or anything else. You can also get online help on how to modify the elements by clicking the letter type icon.

SAVE THE FILE

Once you are finished, you can save your work as a new Word template by selecting <u>FILE/SAVE</u> and choosing <u>Word template</u> as the format you wish to save the document in. This modified template will be available to you any time, saved in Word's default Template folder. Templates can be created from any document and not just from previous templates. There is no point in saving a document as a template, however, unless you have done something in the basic layout of the file that you will want to use for a lot of other files. It's a good idea to have a separate template for each type of file you use — personal letter templates as well as business letter templates, for example.

THE GOLDEN RULES...

There are several vital things you need to know and remember at all times. One of them is to back up your work! There are few feelings worse in the world of computing than to spend hours preparing a document only to lose it all because of a power failure or computer crash.

Make sure you press Ctrl+O at frequent intervals. Doing that will "Quick Save" your work, saving your document without slowing you down too much – and in all seriousness, we recommend doing so every few minutes. To provide further protection, Word 2000 has a useful inbuilt security feature called AutoRecover that makes automatic backups of the files that you are working on. To change the settings for saving, open the comprehensive options window by clicking

AutoRecover will provide you with another backup in case of power failure or any other problem. You can set the interval time between saves.

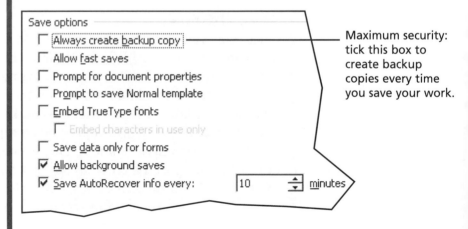

Save options

☐ Always create backup copy
☐ Allow fast saves
☐ Prompt for document properties
☐ Prompt to save Normal template
☐ Embed TrueType fonts
   ☐ Embed characters in use only
☐ Save data only for forms
☑ Allow background saves
☑ Save AutoRecover info every: 10 ⬆⬇ minutes

Maximum security: tick this box to create backup copies every time you save your work.

TOOLS/OPTIONS in the menu bar and then selecting the Save Tab. Ticking the Always Create Backup Copy box will make sure that every time you save your document, the old version will be saved as well, as YOURFILENAME.bak, where your document is called YOURFILENAME.doc. If you accidentally save a document with a problem in it – and it can be easy to miss an error, or to save by mistake – then this can be invaluable. Ticking the Allow Background Saves box will help you to work more smoothly by saving your document while you continue to work, rather than making you wait until Word has finished. Allow Fast Saves lets Word save your work by adding the changes you have made to the end of the previous version of the document. While this is a lot faster than recreating the entire save file, it does make your save files a lot bigger, and tricky to transport. If you have made some large-scale changes to your document, you may also want to save it with a different (or at least slightly modified) name to reflect the new version – and to make sure that if you change your mind later, the old version is still available.

BACKING UP

Being secure about protecting your work also involves making extra copies on floppy disks, Zip disks or even CDs. At the end of every day, you should ideally make a copy of your work on an external drive or other removable storage device of some sort, which you should keep in a different location to your computer – at home, in the office safe, in someone else's office – anywhere away from your hard disk. This may seem over the top, and will often be vaguely inconvenient, but the fact remains that thieves usually take all available floppy disks, Zips and CDs when they steal a computer system, and a fire is equally indiscriminate. If your documents and data would be difficult, time-consuming or expensive to replace, then you want to make absolutely sure you're not going to lose them if the worst happens. There's a saying that goes: "You don't know the value of what you have until you've lost it". You don't really want to find out the true value of your documents the hard way, do you?

SAFETY WHEN SAVING

When you save a file, make sure you are not trying to overwrite an earlier piece of work. If you do, the earlier version will be lost for ever. In case of a file naming conflict – the computing term for when you try to overwrite one file with another – Word will present you with a message asking you if you are really sure you want to go ahead with overwriting the old version. If this message does pop up, it is well worth checking your files, maybe even cancelling the save operation and looking for the file that is being overwritten. Open it, check it and decide whether or not you can afford to do without it for evermore. If not, save your current work with a different name. It's not a lot of time to save yourself a lot of trouble.

UNDO AND REDO

Word offers you the possibility of correcting your mistakes at any time. Clicking the <u>Undo</u> icon (or typing Ctrl + Z) will undo the last action. Whenever anything goes wrong, no matter how bad it seems, try Undo **immediately** – before saving, loading or anything else. The icon next to it, <u>Redo</u>, works in the same way but with the opposite effect – undoing the undo, so to speak.

The much-used <u>Undo</u> and <u>Redo</u> icons.

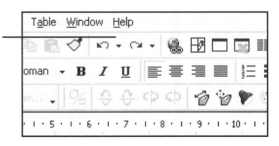

HELP ME

The last Golden Rule is to use all the help you can get. Word 2000 comes with a very effective Help system and an Office Assistant, both sitting or your desktop. There is more on getting Help from the Microsoft Office later in this book.

DOCUMENTS

2

Now that you know how to start new documents and are aware of the basics involved in using Word, we will show you how to produce attractive, effective text using a variety of tools, including how to shape your words according to your needs, draw attention to particular items, and add headers and footers. Moving text around and manipulating layout is probably the biggest innovation that word processors have offered to the writer – power as never before over your documents.

FORMATTING CHARACTERS

Word 2000 offers you a wide range of tools to enhance the visibility and readability of your document. It will let you decide what the entire document or a particular word – even a single letter – will look like.

THE BASIC CONTROLS

You can access all the basic format controls from the dropdown menus in your document's work window.

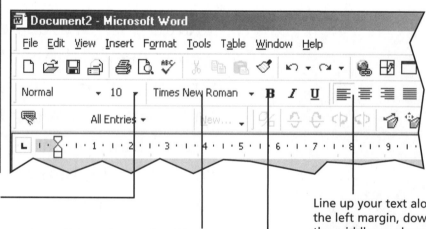

Choose the size of the text (either selected or that you are about to type) here.

Choose the typeface (font) you wish to apply or use from this drop down list.

Use or apply **Bold** *Italic* or <u>Underlined</u> formatting with these icons.

Line up your text along the left margin, down the middle, or along the right margin, or justify it (line it up along both the left and right by spacing the words in each line).

Using these formatting elements is the first stage towards really tailoring a document to its purpose, by highlighting key words or headers. Fonts are a very effective tool as they can really make the difference to the tone that is conveyed:

Dear Sir

Times New Roman: refined and stylish

Hi there!

Comic Sans: much more fun!

MORE FONT OPTIONS

There are a number of ways of attracting the reader's attention to a piece of text, in addition to simply putting it in a different font or underlining it. Selecting some text and clicking the right button on your mouse will bring up a new window. New options to transform and even animate your selected text are available by selecting <u>Font</u> from this list of options.

1 Right-click on some selected text and choose the <u>Fonts</u> option to open the <u>Font</u> dialog box.

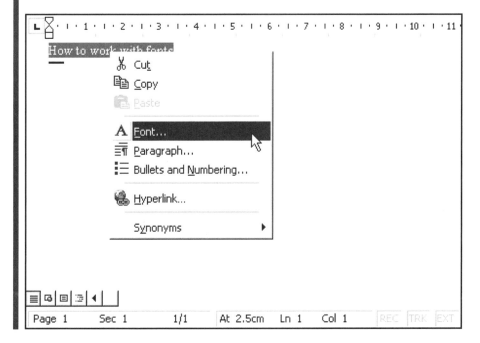

2 Adjust the style of the text you have currently highlighted by using as many of the options as you think you'll need.

Select this tab to modify the way the letters fit together.

Select this tab to play around with fonts and standard effects.

Select this tab to alter the way the text is displayed.

Pick the font you wish to use here.

Make your text bigger or smaller.

Select the style you need.

Select the colour of your text, the way it is going to be underlined and the colour of the underline.

You can tick on any number of boxes to apply multiple effects, although some options cancel one another out.

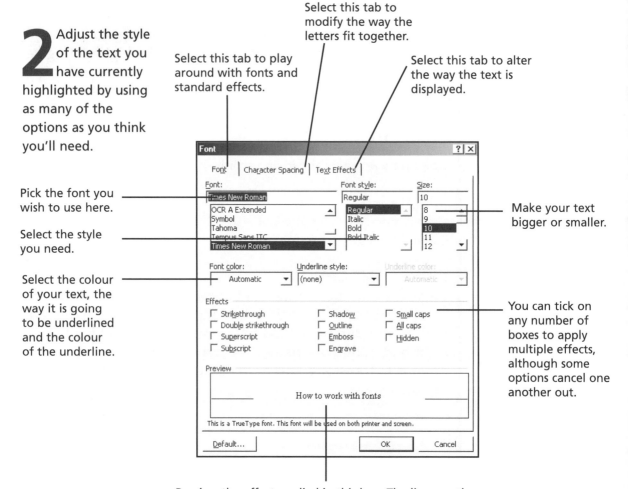

Preview the effect applied in this box. The lines on the side will show you where the text is going to be typed in respect to the baseline, the default position for text.

SERIF OR NOT SERIF?

Text fonts come in three major families, Serif, Sans Serif (i.e. no serifs), and Script (handwriting style). Serifs are the small bars that terminate major lines within each letter.

This is written in a Serif font...

...while this is written in a Sans Serif font...

...and this is written in a Script font.

FONT EFFECTS

In addition to the font effects listed on the previous page, there are many more effects and styles that you can apply to your text by selecting the Text Effects tab of the Fonts dialog box. You can add a flashing background to your text, add a number of different moving surrounds, or even cover it with an overlay of stars or shimmers.

1 Using the Text Effects tab, you can choose a special effect for your text. A preview appears in the window as you select the effect.

DEFAULTING A STYLE

The Default button is a risky one: clicking it will apply the font, styles and effects you have just chosen to *all* the work that will be based on the Normal template – the default blank document. This template probably forms the basis of most of your work later on, so you should be very sure that you like a font or an effect before you click on this button. It is safer and probably more sensible to just adjust your fonts and special effects on a document-by-document basis. However, using the Default button will not affect the work based on any other templates, which will remain untouched.

USING SPECIAL CHARACTERS

There will be times when you will need to insert special characters such as currency or copyright symbols, or accented foreign letters. You can do that by choosing INSERT/ SYMBOLS from the main menu bar.

1 Click on Symbols in the INSERT menu to bring up this box.

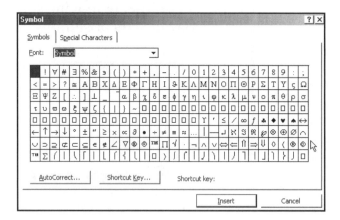

2 Choose the symbol that you want to use by clicking on it and then pressing the Insert button.

FONT

Select the font you need. The default font is Symbol. If you select any other one, the characters available within that particular font will appear in the grid below. The options that you have available will depend on the fonts that you have installed on your system.

CHARACTER

Click on the character you need and a larger size preview will pop up. Once you have clicked on a character, you can navigate through the other characters with the cursor keys.

INSERT

This button will insert the symbol selected in the text you are currently working on, at the position your cursor is in.

SHORTCUT KEY...

Some symbols already have a shortcut key assigned to them. These will be shown here: type the key or combination and the symbol will be inserted. You can assign your own shortcut key to any symbol, or modify an existing one. Here's how to do it.

CREATING A NEW SHORTCUT

1 First, make sure you are preparing a shortcut for the correct symbol, as previewed.

2 Type in the combination of keys you wish to use when you have clicked in the <u>Press new shortcut key</u> box.

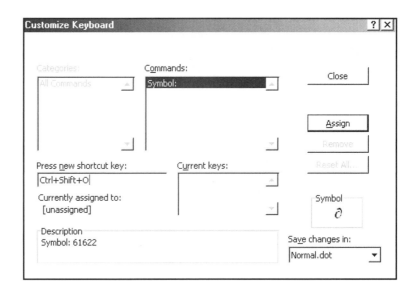

3 Click the <u>Close</u> button to get back to your document.

If you find that a symbol already has a selection that you don't want, just click in the <u>Current Keys</u> box and overtype your preferred keystrokes. When you have chosen your key, you can save the changes either in the Normal template (and therefore make this shortcut key available for all the work you will do later using a blank document) or only in the current document. You can choose which you want to do in the <u>Save changes in</u> dropdown menu. There are other ways to insert characters – each character in a set has a specific number. You can note this number down and, later, hold down <u>Alt</u> and type the full number – from the keypad only, not the main number bar – instead of creating a shortcut key.

MAKE IT COUNT

It is a good idea to try to create a combination of keys that have some kind of relation to the symbol you are working on – such as <u>Ctrl+Alt+Shift+I</u> for the infinity symbol. If you have a lot of keystrokes, it can get confusing.

The <u>Special characters</u> tab of the <u>Symbols</u> dialog gives you a list of special characters you can insert. You can still change their shortcut keys if you want to.

SELECTING TEXT

To apply a style or a special effect to some text you have already typed, or to move it around, you need to select it. This can be easily done with the mouse: click where you want the selection to start, and keep the button down while dragging until you reach the point you want the selection to stop. Selected text will appear highlighted.

MORE SHORTCUTS

Word 2000 also has a series of shortcut keys that make selecting more accurate. All the cursor keys (See Page 18) can be used to select text if they are pressed with the Shift key. For example Shift+Ctrl+Left arrow will select the whole word after the cursor.

Who will be the New Bishop?

In he latter days of July in the year 185—, a most important question was for ten days hourly asked in the cathedral city of Barchester, and answered every hour in various ways — Who was to be the new Bishop?

The death of old Dr Grantly, who had for many years filled that chair with meek authority, took place even as the ministry of Lord — was going

You can select a whole line by placing your mouse at the beginning of that line. When the pointer changes to a white arrow, click to highlight.

Once you have selected a section of text, you can modify it in a number of ways. Click anywhere in your highlighted text with your right button and check the options available – be careful though: clicking on any section of highlighted text with the left button will deselect the text!

1 Click on the right button of the mouse when the pointer is in a selection of text: this useful dropdown menu appears.

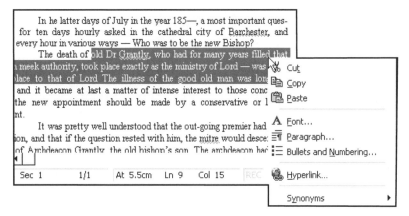

The greatest feature of all for any word processor must be the ability to delete, copy and move text around. This is easily achieved in Word and it is very fast. The most common way to do it is with the mouse: select some text, place your cursor anywhere in the selection and left-click, holding the button down. Move the cursor to where you want the text to move to, then release. You might need to practice to get the hang of it: the first few times you may just deselect the whole thing if you do not hold the button down, or bring up the paragraph formatting popup menu if you use the right button.

If you select a portion of text and type something, the selection will be overwritten and replaced with what you have just typed. This feature is very powerful – and useful – as it enables you to modify your text rapidly, but it can also mean that you delete large chunks of text easily too. Don't forget about the all-important Undo command!

Undo and Redo. Click on the arrows to access menus.

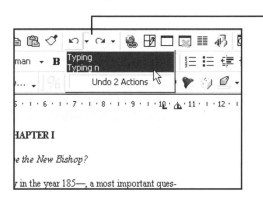

1 Click on the arrow on the right of the Undo or Redo icon to drop down a menu with a text modification history.

KEYBOARD SELECTION

You can also play around with a selection using the keyboard. Ctrl+X will cut the selection (remove it from your work) and place it on the clipboard for you to use later. Ctrl+C will copy the selection to the clipboard while Ctrl+V will paste the contents of the clipboard to wherever you wish. These functions can also be accessed by clicking EDIT/CUT, EDIT/COPY or EDIT/PASTE in the main menu bar, or by right-clicking once in a selection. The contents of the clipboard will always be inserted at the current cursor position unless the Overwrite option is on. Another shortcut you can use is a rather drastic one – Ctrl+A will select all the text and apply whatever transformation you wish to the whole of the document. Including Delete. Use it carefully.

THE CLIPBOARD

Word 2000 has a new type of "active" clipboard that can hold up to 12 selections. As soon as you Copy or Cut more than once, your successive selections will be available in the Clipboard Viewer, which will pop up straight away. To insert a clipboard selection into your text, first click where you need this selection to go. Then place your mouse over one of the Word page icons in the Clipboard Viewer for a second or so. The first 50 characters of the content will be displayed in a screen tip box underneath the icon, as shown next page. When you have made your choice, simply click and the selected clipboard extract will be pasted into your document where your cursor sits. This is one of the really handy new features of Word 2000 because it means that, unlike other programs, text that has been cut doesn't just disappear once it has been used and copied over.

NEW WAY TO CLIP   ▬ ▢ ✕

When you Cut or Copy text, you put the selection in the clipboard. The clipboard is a portion of your computer's memory or hard disk that can store a wide variety of data. This data can be retrieved later on by the program, or even by another application that accepts the same kind of data.

This button will paste the contents of all items on the clipboard one after the other, in the order they have been gathered.

1 When you have Cut or Copied more than once, the Clipboard Viewer will automatically appear.

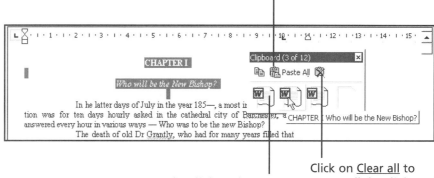

The clipboard can hold up to twelve successive selections.

Click on Clear all to empty all the clipboard. You can't delete or move individual items.

Not just the words are transferred to the clipboard when you Copy or Cut. Any formatting that the text had will be saved for future use too. For instance, Bold or Italic text put into the clipboard will still be pasted back as Bold or Italic, although the formatting will not appear in the screen tip box when you hover over a clipboard icon.

Word also adds or gets rid of extra spaces at the beginning and the end of a copied text so that when you paste it, you don't end up with words stuck to one another, or miles away from one another. This feature is called Smart Cut and Paste and to check whether it's on, or to disable it, open the TOOLS/OPTION/EDIT tab.

If you do not wish to see the Clipboard Viewer, you can hide it by deselecting the VIEW/TOOLBAR/CLIPBOARD selection box.

FORMATTING AND UNFORMATTING

If you need to get rid of a formatting style…
Press Ctrl+Spacebar to remove the formatting style of the word under the cursor.
Press Ctrl+Shift+Z to remove all formatting styles in the whole of the document (you may want to think twice about this, or to rush to the Undo icon after this one…)

SEARCHING AND REPLACING

From time to time you will need to find a particular word in your document. If you are typing a short letter it's no big deal, but if you need to search a 200,000-word report that runs to hundreds of pages, it could take some time. Fortunately, Word 2000 comes with very powerful search and replace functions that can change single or multiple instances of a word into something else.

EASY TO FIND

The simplest funtion when searching and selecting is the basic Find function. It is accessed through the Find dialog, using the shortcut Ctrl+F, or from EDIT/FIND in the menu bar.

1 Bring up the Find dialog box, accessed from the EDIT menu.

Find and Replace	? X
Find	Replace	Go To
Find what:	
Format: Double underline	
More ∓	Find Next	Cancel

Type the word or string of characters you are looking for in the Find what box. This is known as the "Search String", a term left over from early computing jargon.

Clicking on the down arrow to the right of the <u>Find Word</u> box shows you a dropdown menu containing your recent queries.

FIND NEXT

Use this button if the word you have just found matching your search is not the *exact* one you need in the document. You will get a message from Word when you reach the end of the document telling you that there is no more text to check.

MORE BUTTON

You can fine-tune your search with a number of options by selecting <u>More</u> and placing a tick in the appropriate box.

2 Click on the <u>More</u> button to bring up a whole host of options, including case matching, wildcards, sound matching, related tenses of the word, and more, described below.

3 Switch the various search options on and off with the check boxes.

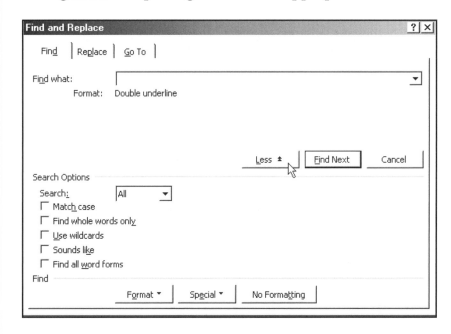

SEARCH

You can search the entire document, or you can search either up or down from the current cursor position, with this box.

MATCH CASE

When selected, your search will be case-sensitive, which would mean that searching for "The" would not find "the" if it was in the document.

FIND WHOLE WORDS ONLY

Your search might return parts of a word, where the search string is present – "there" will be found in both "there" and "thereafter" for instance. A tick in this box will limit your search to matching only a whole word to your search string.

USE WILDCARDS

A wildcard is a special character that has a special function in a search string. If you want to use wildcards, tick this box, click on the <u>Special</u> button and pick the wildcard you need, or type a wildcard character in the <u>Find what</u> box. If this box is not ticked and the search string contains wildcard characters, they will be treated as plain text (ordinary characters) instead.

SOUNDS LIKE

This option will return words that sound like the search string. Be careful though: the results can be unpredictable sometimes!

FIND ALL WORD FORMS

This is a powerful feature. It will replace all forms of a word, especially verbs, with those of another. If you want to replace the verb "choose" with the verb "select", with this option active, "chosen" will be replaced by "selected" too. All declensions of the word are changed, not just the "root" form. This option is to be used with the <u>Find and Replace</u> feature described in the following pages..

1 To broaden your search to formatted text, hit the <u>Format</u> button. A series of options of search criteria appears.

2 Clicking <u>Font...</u> brings up the <u>Find font</u> dialog box. Use this to search for formatted text.

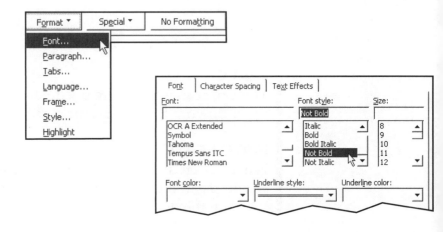

1 <u>Find and Replace</u> is as simple as <u>Find</u>. Just add a text string to replace your text with.

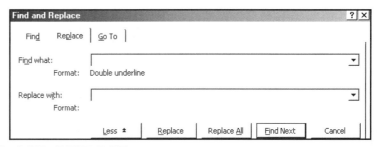

FIND AND REPLACE

To replace one word – or a string of characters – with another, proceed as for a normal search. Open the <u>Replace</u> window with your mouse (<u>Edit/Replace</u> in the main window) or use the shortcut <u>Ctrl+H</u>. Fill in the blank boxes, and click on one of the buttons. <u>Replace</u> lets you choose one word at a time to replace, while <u>Replace All</u> will process the whole document. <u>Find Next</u> lets you navigate your document just to have a look for any instances of the word you may need to replace.

REPLACING FORMATTING

You can search and replace not only plain text, but formatted text too. Use the <u>Format</u> button in the <u>Find and Replace</u> window (see page 36) to select the options you want to take into account while searching and replacing. To replace all the text formatted with a particular style, leave the search and replace fields empty, selecting format only. All the text in Double Underline in the example above will be replaced by plain text. You can set the style of your search/replace by clicking in the <u>Find What</u> and <u>Replace With</u> fields respectively.

GO TO IT

The last tab in the <u>Find and Replace</u> window is <u>Go To</u>. Use it to move around your document or to find things you've lost.

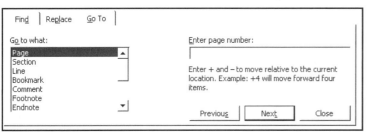

Select the type of marker you want to go to (e.g. a page or section), enter identifying information such as a page number and click <u>Next</u>.

HEADERS AND FOOTERS

Another way to give your text a more professional touch is by adding headers or footers to it. A header is a line of information that appears at the top of your printed page, while a footer goes at the bottom. The most common use for a footer is to show page numbers or print dates. Word 2000 has a collection of useful information you can add just at the click of a button. Here is how it is done:

A footer on a formal letter will look professional and can be very handy to help you keep track of your work.

Click on <u>View</u> in the main menu bar and choose <u>View Header and Footer</u>.

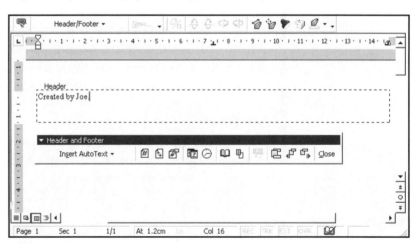

The header for your first page will be displayed in a dotted line box. Type your header in this box. If you scroll down to the end of your page, you will notice a similar box, this time for the footer. The <u>Header and Footer</u> toolbar also appears on your screen. From there you are able to access several functions to insert pre-formatted information, and navigate your headers and footers.

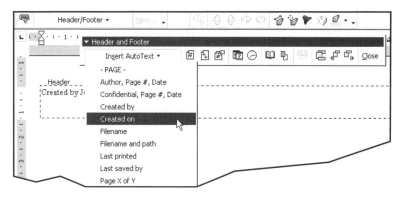

INSERT AUTOTEXT
Clicking this button will provide you with a dropdown menu containing the most-used information for headers and footers. Select an item and it will be added at the text cursor.

ICONS
The row of icons (below) contains fields that can be incorporated in your header or footer. Clicking on one of them will insert the relevant item at the current cursor location.

CLOSE
Closing this toolbar will also close the <u>Header and Footer</u> editing view.

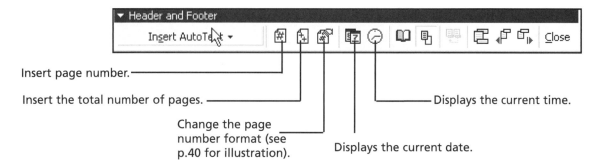

Insert page number.

Insert the total number of pages.

Change the page number format (see p.40 for illustration).

Displays the current date.

Displays the current time.

To change page number display styles, select the format you need from the dropdown list. Your options include standard numerals, reference letters, roman numerals and more.

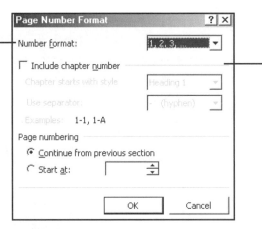

This option will add the chapter number. It will only work if you have used Word 2000's <u>Bullet and Numbering</u> function (See Page 52).

HEADERS AND FOOTERS FOR SEPARATE SECTIONS

You can change the numbering between different sections of a document, say between an introduction and the main text proper. A Section Break is like a line break, inserted to cut the document into separate parts. To start a new section, place your cursor where you want the section to be and select <u>Insert/Break</u> from the main menu. Select the type of break you wish to insert (generally <u>Continuous</u>) and click <u>OK</u>:

You can specify the way the new section is going to behave by activating the radio buttons.

Once this is done, click somewhere in the section that needs a different page numbering format and open the <u>Header and Footer</u> window again (<u>View/Header and Footer</u> in the main menu). Click on the page number format icon again and perform all the necessary changes. Your page numbering will be updated straight away. You can repeat this operation as often as you like although, as the name of the game is trying to create clear and easily readable documents, it might not be advisable to muddy your document with too many different styles of page numbers.

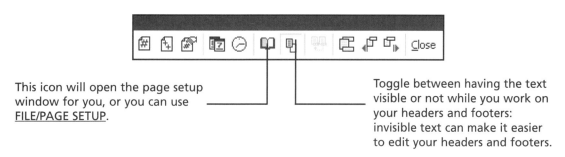

This icon will open the page setup window for you, or you can use FILE/PAGE SETUP.

Toggle between having the text visible or not while you work on your headers and footers: invisible text can make it easier to edit your headers and footers.

SET IT ALL UP

You can modify most elements of your document. Select FILE/PAGE SETUP to modify how your document size and margins will look and where the headers and footers will be placed.

1 Select where the new section is going to start in the Page Setup box.

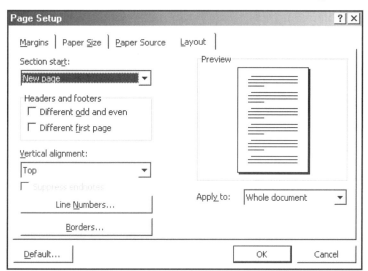

2 Specify the part of your document this setup will apply to in Apply to.

HEADER AND FOOTER LAYOUT

You can have a different header and footer for the first page of your document, and/or have different ones for odd and even pages. The Headers and Footers radio buttons will do just that.

The Preview window is useful to check the layout of your document once the various options available have been applied to it. If you move to the Margins tab, you can specify how wide your headers and footers will be by modifying the amount of page space they are assigned.

The values in the <u>From Edge</u> box, displayed in the <u>Margins</u> tab of the <u>Page Setup</u> dialog box, will let you modify the positions of your headers and footers:

1 Modify the placement of your headers and footers from the top and bottom edges of your page by either typing in a value or using the arrows to increment or decrement the value.

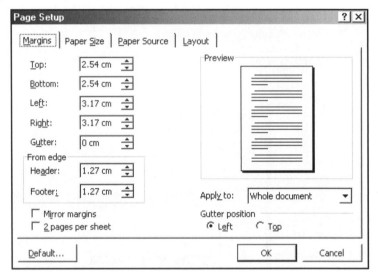

OTHER DIALOGS

These extra icons are available for your use on the Header and Footer toolbar.

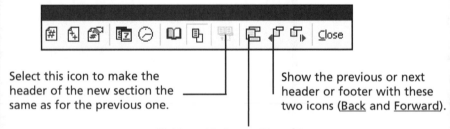

Select this icon to make the header of the new section the same as for the previous one.

Show the previous or next header or footer with these two icons (<u>Back</u> and <u>Forward</u>).

Clicking this icon will toggle between header and footer.

If you only need headers or footers to display a page number, you can use the <u>Page Number</u> function instead by selecting <u>INSERT/ PAGE NUMBER</u> from the menu bar.

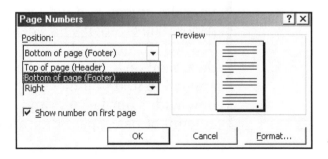

GETTING MORE FROM WORD

3

Once the basic formatting and layout of your text has been settled, it's time to consider some of the other elements that go into a good document. In this chapter, we'll look at using tabs, changing the spacing between lines and characters, and in general tuning up your document so that the information it contains is clear and easily accessible. The use of bullets, lists, columns and colours will also be discussed, along with a wide range of effects such as adding borders and shading to your work.

PARAGRAPH FORMATTING

The keys to formatting paragraphs are tabs. A tab is a way of moving the text on the page in a properly ordered manner. You will need them when you want sections or sentences to start anywhere other than right up against the margin – with lists or indents, for example. Hit the <u>Tab</u> key on your keyboard and watch the cursor jump a block: that's a Word 2000 default tab stop – a gap of one inch.

TABBING AND STOPPING

Tab stops occur at regular intervals of one inch (2.54cm) by default, and mark the left-hand edge of the text. Inserting a tab into your text makes the following character start at the next tab stop position. This will often be fine for your needs. If you do want to modify this – if, for example, you want to prepare a custom list – it is easy to add a new tab stop. To insert a tab stop, first check you can see the ruler at the top of your document, then select the text you want to apply the new tab stop to and click on the ruler at the position you want the new tab to be in, or, if you want to move the tab stop, click on it and drag it to its new position. If you want to get rid of it, simply drag it all the way down and out of the ruler. Note that a stop has no effect unless there are tabs in the document. Tabs are also great for creating quick tables – space your items out with tabs rather than spaces, and you can then highlight the text and drag tab stops to get the table lined up.

Select the type of tab stop here – lining up to the left, centre or right, as shown in this image.

The decimal point of any series of numbers will be centred on this tab stop.

This tab works like a typewriter by aligning your text after it.

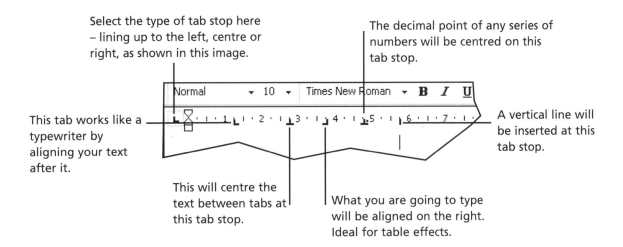

A vertical line will be inserted at this tab stop.

This will centre the text between tabs at this tab stop.

What you are going to type will be aligned on the right. Ideal for table effects.

Usefully, a tab can be assigned a **leader**. A leader is a line of dots or dashes that fills in the tab space, to show how things line up across the page. To assign a leader to a tab stop, either go to <u>FORMAT/TABS</u> in the main menu bar, or double-click on the tab stop you want to modify.

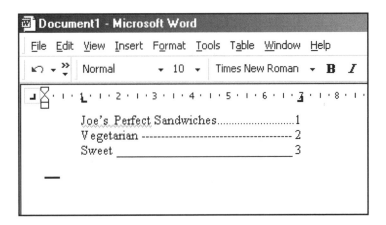

Here is an example of the leaders you can assign to a tab stop. As you can see, a couple of tabs and a leader can produce a simple but effective table.

1 Select the Tabs dialog box from the FORMAT menu to adjust everything you could possibly want to, including adding a leader line.

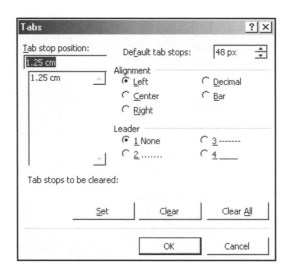

TAB STOP POSITION
Use this box to select the position of the tab stop you want to modify.

DEFAULT TAB STOPS
Specify the space between Word's default tabs.

ALIGNMENT
Select the type of alignment for this particular tab stop.

LEADER
Select the type of leader any given tab stop will have.

SET
Use this button to set a new tab stop through this window.

CLEAR AND CLEAR ALL
If you are not happy with the tab stop adjustments you have made, clear them individually or collectively with this button.

THE TABS PROPERTY BOX
You can use the tabs property box to enter numerical values for the exact positioning of your tab stops, as well as deleting some of or all of them. For example, if you create a tab stop by

double clicking on the ruler, but it is not in quite the right place, double-click on the tab, note its position, and in the Tab stop position box type the correct position and click on Set. The new tab stop will take effect. You can now safely click on the previous tab stop in the list and click Clear, replacing one tab stop with another.

CHARACTER SPACING

A word that appears on a line on its own on a line at the end of a paragraph is an Orphan. This paragraph terminates in an Orphan.

One of the ways to correct orphans, which look sloppy, is to change the spacing between the letters themselves. This can also be useful under other circumstances. By adjusting this value, the word (or words, paragraphs or pages) you select can be made wider or narrower on a line-by-line basis. Select Fonts from the FORMAT menu, and click on the Character Spacing tab. You can use the Scale value to change the actual display size of the font, or select Expanded or Contracted from the Spacing picklist and then add a point value (including fractions) to widen or shrink the font. The Position value changes the relative position of two lines in the paragraph.

```
┌─────────────────────────────────────────────────────┐
│ Font                                           ? │ X │
├─────────────────────────────────────────────────────┤
│                                                       │
│   Font    │ Character Spacing │ Text Effects │        │
│                                                       │
│   Scale:      100%        ▼                           │
│                                                       │
│   Spacing:    Normal          ▼    By:     ▲▼         │
│                                                       │
│   Position:   Normal          ▼    By:     ▲▼         │
│                                                       │
│   □ Kerning for fonts:        ▲▼  Points and above    │
└─────────────────────────────────────────────────────┘
```

If you tick the Kerning option, you will tell Word 2000 to **kern** the characters – that is, to reduce the space between certain letters, such as "l" and "i". The Points and Above box shows at what size the letters are kerned. Here's what the options do:

SCALE
Resizes your text. You can use the arrow on the right to select a scale preset, or type in your own values.

SPACING
Modifies the spacing between each selected letter.

POSITION
Changes the position of your text above or below the baseline.

KERNING FOR FONTS
Turns the extra kerning functions on or off.

It is best to apply character spacing to at least one line or paragraph. If you do not, your text will look odd, seemingly appearing to be shrunk together or b l o w n u p compared to the rest of the text.

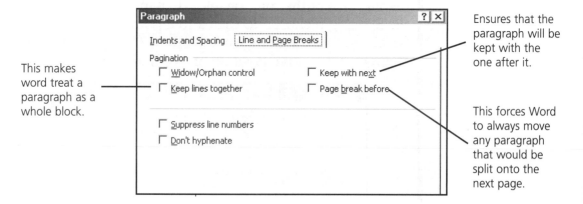

This makes word treat a paragraph as a whole block.

Ensures that the paragraph will be kept with the one after it.

This forces Word to always move any paragraph that would be split onto the next page.

Word 2000 can take care of quite a lot of character formatting for you. Open the paragraph formatting window by clicking on FORMAT/PARAGRAPH from the menu bar and clicking on the Line and Page Break tab. The Pagination options all work to make your text look better in different ways – Widows/Orphan Control stops Word leaving single lines floating messily at the top or bottom of the page, for example.

1 Select quick line spacing from the dropdown list on the <u>Indents and Spacing</u> tab, or type <u>Ctrl+1</u> for single, <u>Ctrl+5</u> for 1.5 and <u>Ctrl+2</u> for double spacing.

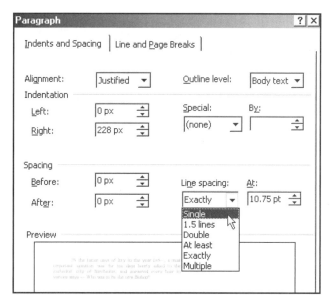

It is possible to modify the vertical line spacing as well as the horizontal letter spacing of a document from the <u>Paragraph</u> dialog. A line spacing set to <u>1.5</u> or to <u>double</u> will make your text clearer. You can of course apply all these modifications to any paragraph you want by highlighting it – leaving the others untouched – or to the whole text or a new paragraph. Double spacing is useful when proofreading printed text, because you can write notes between the lines.

INDENTING

Moving whole paragraphs left or right will draw your readers' attention to particular points or ideas in your document and help structure your work. This is called indenting. The easiest way to indent a paragraph (by one tab stop) is to select it and click the <u>Increase indent</u> icon. If you want more indent, do so again. If it is too indented, click the <u>Decrease indent</u> icon until the text is where it is supposed to go. Quotes are traditionally indented, for example.

1 The Increase and Decrease indent icons are located on the <u>Formatting</u> toolbar.

Decrease indent

Increase indent

The following pictures will show you some of the different indents you can create. The first one is a simple, no frills indent. At the top of your document, where the ruler sits, you will notice a set of two grey arrows...

1 The paragraph control handle shows – and affects – the paragraph's indents

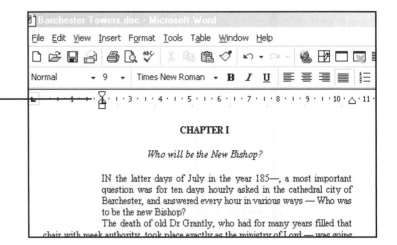

If you want a whole paragraph indent, move the bottom arrow on the left to the position you want the first and subsequent lines to start (as above).

2 This is how not to do a first line indent! The guiding rule of formatting is that if it looks ugly, it is probably wrong.

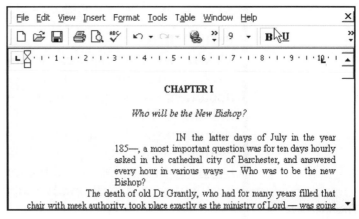

A first line indent is when the first line of a paragraph starts on the right of the text. You do this by moving the top arrow on the left-hand control to the position that you want the first line to start at.

3 This is a rather extreme hanging indent. Hanging indents are generally used in bulleted lists.

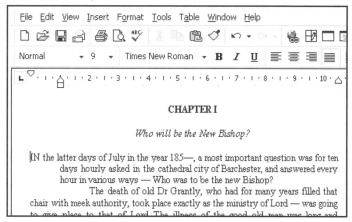

If you want to create a hanging indent – the opposite of a first line indent – indent the paragraph to the right using the bottom arrow and then move the top arrow to the left to where you want the hanging indent to start.

4 You can also apply a right-hand indent using the right paragraph control.

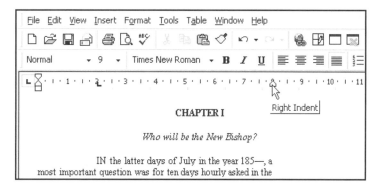

The arrow on the right (the right indent) can be used to **nest** a paragraph – that is, to indent it on the right. All these indents can be further adjusted by assigning them a numerical value in the Paragraph Formatting window, which can be accessed via FORMAT/PARAGRAPH from the main menu bar.

QUICK KEY FOR MENUS

Instead of using a right click to access the menus, you can hit the Menu key, which is next to the Start key on your keyboard – it is the one with the drawing of a mouse pointer clicking on a menu – while your cursor is in a selected piece of text.

BULLET LISTS AND COLUMNS

Bullets and lists are a great way to:

- Itemize several separate but linked points;
- Establish a clear order or ranking;
- Summarize information from a section;
- Draw attention to key issues; and
- Make your text more accessible.

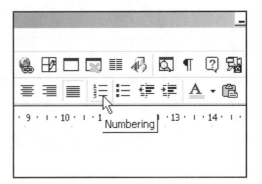

BULLET BASICS

Just as with everything else in Word, there are multiple ways to access bullets and numbered lists. The most straightforward way is from the icons in the tool bar. The numbered list icon is the one with the cursor over it in the image above. The icon to the right of it is the bullet list icon. A numbered list, like the one that starts this section, has each item beginning with a number, suggesting priority. In a bullet list, each item starts with an abstract symbol, such as a circle, square or star. This avoids suggesting a firm order, and can look more attractive.

1 While the <u>Bullet</u> and <u>Number</u> list icons switch the default options on or off for your text, greater control is available by selecting the <u>Bullets and Numbering</u> option from the right-click pick-list, or from the <u>Format</u> menu. In all cases though, select your text first!

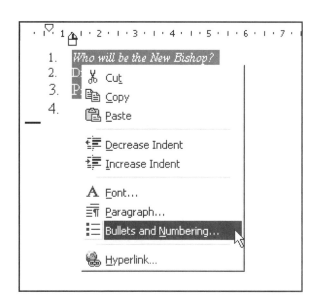

2 The <u>Bullets and Numbering</u> dialog allows you to select your bullet type on the tab shown, or to select a type of numbered list from the <u>Numbered</u> tab. Click on the tab and then the style you want, and then on <u>OK</u>, For <u>Outline Numbered</u> lists, apply the list and then press tab once at the start of the line for each item you want to become a sub-clause.

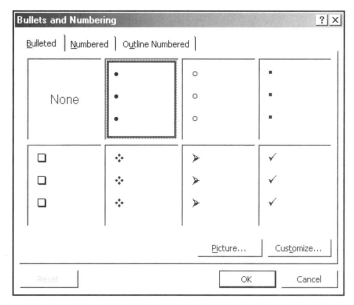

THE BULLET BOX
Using the large examples in the <u>Bulleted</u> tab, you can choose one of seven standard layouts for your bulleted lists. If you are not happy with these standard offerings, use <u>Customize</u> to create your own. You can include any symbol from any font as a bullet, and even a piece of clip art.

1 Clicking on Customize in the Bulleted tab brings up this box – the Customize Bulleted List dialog.

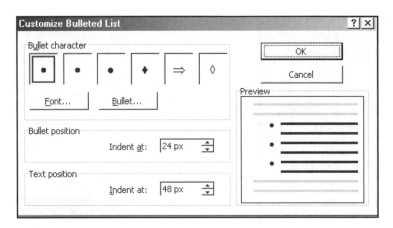

BULLET... BUTTON
The default font set that Word 2000 will look in for bullet symbols will be the Symbol Font set, but some font sets (such as Wingdings) are made exclusively of special characters you can use as bullets. You can choose your bullet character from your range of available fonts with this button. Pick a bullet from this list that appears by double-clicking on a character, or choose a different font by clicking on the font name and selecting a new one from the dropdown list.

FONT... BUTTON
Once you have chosen your bullet, you can modify its attributes, including the size, colour and style, with the standard formatting controls this button invokes.

PREVIEW
A picture of the current bullet style is shown in this window.

BULLET INDENT
Specify how far in the bullets are going to be indented here.

TEXT INDENT
Specify how far the text is going to be indented here. Note that the text indent has to be larger than the bullet indent, and for best effect, the difference between them should be bigger than the width of the bullet character itself.

1 Open the <u>Numbered</u> list, tab from the dialog on page 53.

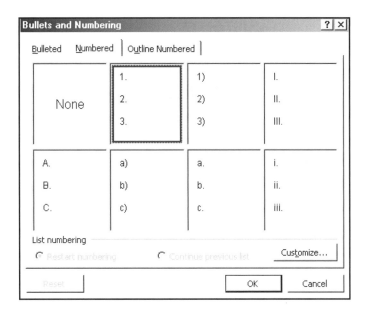

NUMBERED LISTS

Clicking on the <u>Numbered</u> tab brings up a selection of numbered lists you can choose from. These work the same way as the <u>Bullet</u> selections.

LIST NUMBERING

One extra option is available if you select – or click within – a single list item inside a number list. You can choose to restart the numbering again from 1 by clicking on the <u>Restart Numbering</u> radio button, or undo this choice by clicking on the <u>Continue previous list</u> button. You can change the numbering style at the same time, so that you can make your list read 1, 2, 3, 4, i, ii, iii, for example. You are however unable to then return to the old list, so you could not automatically make Word number the item after iii as 5 without choosing <u>customize</u>. If you want to nest lists like this, use <u>Outline Numbered lists</u> instead, which are designed for such use. Outline lists work on a hierarchy basis, and can be set to have all types of sub-clauses within a single list. They are selected and modified in the same was as normal numbered lists. Note though that items are demoted (ie made into a sub-clause) by pressing tab at the start of the line to demote.

CUSTOMIZE

Selecting the <u>Customize</u> button lets you modify the various options and details of your numbered list:

Use the <u>Customize Numbered List</u> dialog to tailor your numbered lists, and click <u>OK</u> when you're happy with the results.

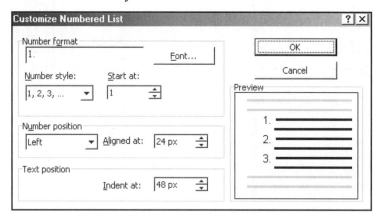

FONT...

This button lets you call up the <u>Font formatting</u> dialog.

NUMBER STYLE

Choose the numbering style from this pick-list, and select the number the list starts at with the <u>Start At</u> value.

NUMBER POSITION

This tells Word how to align the numbers in the list – along the left hand side, the right hand side, or in the centre.

ALIGNED AT/INDENT AT

These values work the same way as their Bullet counterparts. Specify how far the item number and item text are going to be indented. As for bullets, the text indent has to be larger than the list number indent, and should be further away from the list number than the width of the largest number your list is going to extend to. If you create an outline list, you should bear in mind that subclauses will be further indented, and their names might get quite long – 1.1.4.3a, for example.

PREVIEW

Check what your list will look like in this box.

COLUMNS

Arranging text in columns is a staple of the journalistic trade. Ideal for newsletters and information sheets, documents with lots of pictures or long lists of short lines (like an index), columns are simple in word. Type your text as normal, then select it and choose <u>Columns</u> from the <u>FORMAT</u> menu to open the <u>Columns</u> dialog. You can apply a preset by selecting it and clicking OK, or you can manually select how many columns you want. In general, keeping them equal width looks best.

You can give your columns more room for text by decreasing the <u>Spacing</u> value, or fill them by increasing it. You can also add a keyline between each column by clicking on the <u>Line between</u> box.

The more columns you have, the smaller your <u>spacing</u> should be. The preview box will show you how your text will look.

TIDYING YOUR COLUMNS

Sometimes, your columns will not line up properly, with one ending only halfway as far down as the one before, or even being totally empty. Word will often take care of this itself automatically – making sure columns are properly distributed is known as balancing – but on occasion you may need to do it manually. To do this, click immediately at the end of the text in the last column and insert a break. Choose <u>INSERT/BREAK</u> from the menu bar, then select <u>Continuous</u> from the <u>Section Break Types</u>. Click <u>OK,</u> and the columns will balance. Note that if you have widow and orphan protection on, you may need to break a paragraph into chunks before the columns will be able to balance evenly.

To add or remove columns, click in the columned text and select <u>FORMAT/COLUMNS</u>. From the dialog box, either select <u>One</u> to return to normal, or make the changes you need.

COLOUR, SHADING AND BORDERS

Although it will not always be appropriate for formal documents, careful use of paragraph borders and boxes, colours and shading can go a long way to breaking up the dense appearance of a text-heavy document. They also let you add emphasis to an important paragraph, or draw attention to key notes.

1 Click anywhere inside the paragraph which you want to modify and then click on the FORMAT/ BORDERS AND SHADING entry in the main menu bar to bring up the window from which you'll be able to add borders and shading effects to that paragraph.

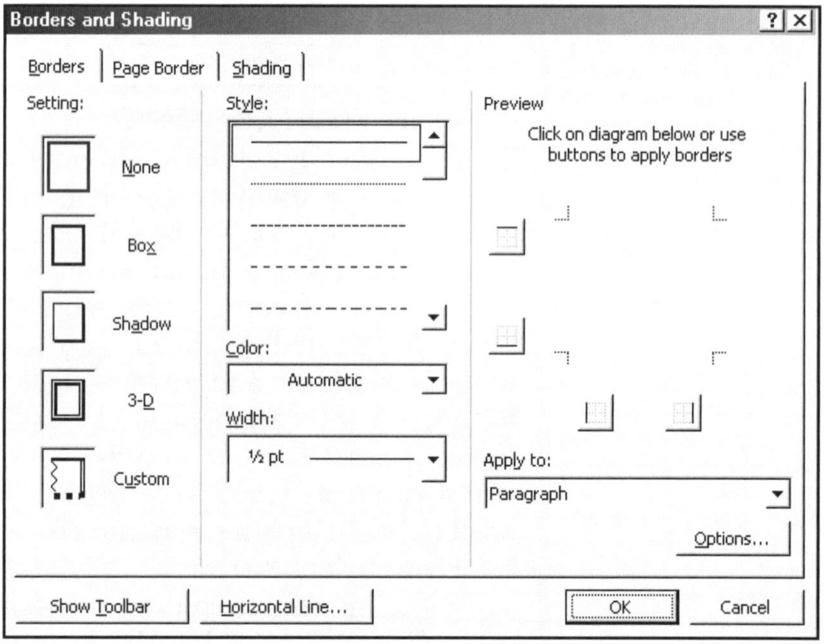

Borders and Shading | ? | X |

Borders | Page Border | Shading

Setting:

None

Box

Shadow

3-D

Custom

Style:

Color:
Automatic

Width:
½ pt

Preview

Click on diagram below or use buttons to apply borders

Apply to:
Paragraph

Options...

Show Toolbar | Horizontal Line... | OK | Cancel

SETTINGS

Applying a border to your selected paragraph or paragraphs is easy. Choose the <u>Borders</u> tab. You can then select from one of the four pre-set border settings down the left-hand side, click on the icons around the <u>Preview</u> to add a line matching current <u>Style</u>, <u>Color</u> and <u>Width</u> selection in the corresponding position, or click on the appropriate position in the <u>Preview</u> itself. To change a particular line, set the <u>Style</u> and other details to the way you want it, and then click its icon or <u>Preview</u> space. You can change the distance of the border from the text with the <u>Options</u> button. If you have more than one paragraph selected, you will have the option to add a horizontal line between them as part of the borders with an icon between the <u>Top</u> and <u>Bottom</u> icons in the preview area. The <u>Horizontal Line</u> button is actually rather out of place, as it inserts a clip-art line graphic. If you want to add a background colour or shade, the <u>Shading</u> tab lets you pick either or both, regardless of whether you have a border as well or not.

2 If you want to add a border to your whole page, you can select different types of line – and even graphical images from the Art picklist (shown to the right) – with the options on the <u>Page Border</u> tab.

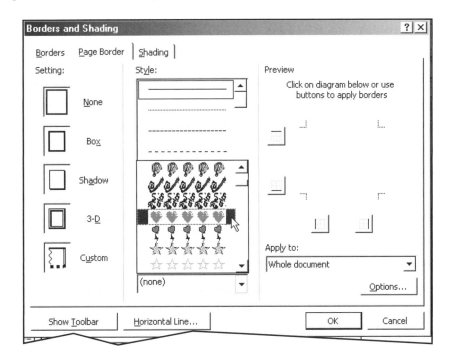

3 Here you can select the colour that you want to apply to the paragraph. Clicking on More Colors will open Windows' colour picker.

You can also give your paragraph a default grey background or a (separately colourable) background pattern from the Style pick-list.

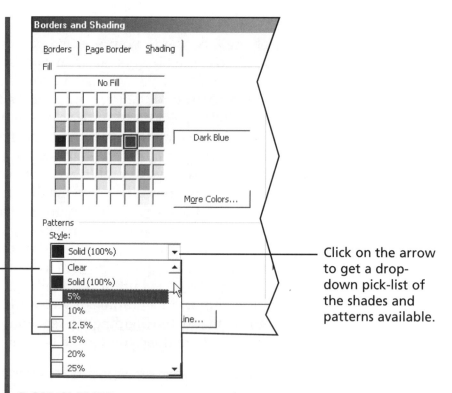

Click on the arrow to get a drop-down pick-list of the shades and patterns available.

BOX CLEVER

Formatting your paragraphs is even easier if you use text boxes. These are little mini-documents that can be placed anywhere in your main document, and you can decide how they interact with the rest of the text in a very detailed way. Note that you have to be in Print Layout view to see text boxes and other drawing objects.

To create a text box, go to INSERT/TEXT BOX from the menu bar. Your mouse pointer will transform itself into a thin cross. Click once to set the top left corner of the box, hold, and drag the box to the correct size, then release. You can now type in the box, apply borders and backgrounds to it, and drag it around and resize it like any other external object by clicking and dragging on the selection box or resize handles, shown below.

Selection box.

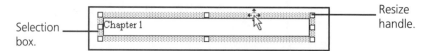

Resize handle.

Once the text box is created, modifying its properties brings you a whole set of tools to enhance its appearance and control its behaviour with the text around it.

1 Access the text box properties window the FORMAT/TEXT box in the main menu bar.

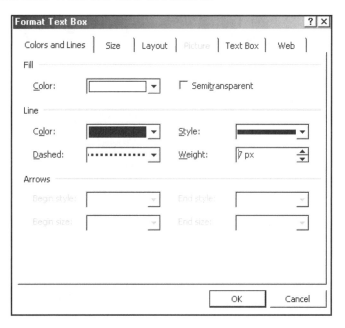

TEXT BOX FORMATTING

Text boxes are extremely versatile, and can be formatted in several ways. The <u>Colors and Lines</u> tab of the <u>Format</u> dialog allows you to format the border and background of the text box itself. Note that <u>No Fill</u> will show the main page through the box, while a <u>White</u> fill will obscure it. You can resize the box from the <u>Size</u> tab, by measurement or percentage, or rotate some text boxes. The <u>Layout</u> tab allows you to specify whether the contents of your text box appear in front of or behind the main page, or to have the text on the main page flow around the box; you can also choose the alignment of the text in the text box here. If you <u>Insert</u> a picture into the text box, you can format that from the <u>Picture</u> tab, which will be greyed out until you do so. The <u>Text Box</u> tab lets you specify how far the text inside the box is from the edges of the box. Finally, the <u>Web</u> tab allows you to specify text to display in the box while pictures inside it are loading – useful for web pages.

SPELLCHECKING AND MORE

To help make sure that your work is as accurate and readable as possible, Word comes with built-in facilities for checking your spelling and grammar. You can perform a full check of your document at any time and sort out problems that may arise, but by default the program examines your work while you type. If it finds a spelling error, it will indicate this by putting a red wavy line under the offending word; if it finds a grammatical error, the wavy line will be green. The spelling checker is usually correct.

CHECK IT OUT

The warning lines will not appear in a printed copy of your work, but it is worth checking red spelling errors. Just click somewhere inside the indicated word and then right-click. The pick-list will start with a range of suggested correct spellings. Select the correct one and the word will be corrected.

As you can see on the left, the list of alternative spellings for you to choose from is in bold. If you typed a non-word, like "hhjhgkjhglk", the first entry will be no suggestion. If what you typed is not misspelled, you can tell Word to ignore all words spelled like this during the current session by clicking Ignore All. If the word is definitely spelled correctly, you can also make the spellchecker learn the new word by clicking on Add. If the word is definitely wrong, you can change all new occurrences of this word, automatically, by clicking on the

AutoCorrect and selecting the right option from the list. If you need to work in a different language, click <u>Language...</u> to see the active languages. <u>Spelling...</u> will let you proceed to a spell check for the entire document (see next page).

1 Select your <u>Default</u> language – the one that the spell checker function will use. This will affect all future work based on the "Normal" template.

The language sets available for this document are listed in the <u>Language</u> menu. Pick the language you want.

Tick this box to cancel continuous spell checking.

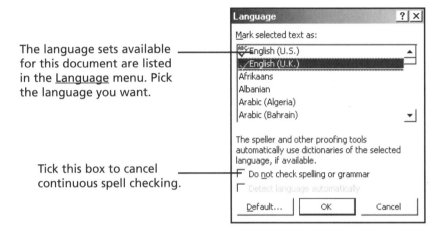

2 To perform a full spell check, click on the <u>Spelling and Grammar</u> icon on the main taskbar

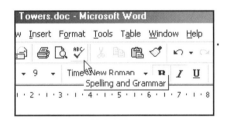

3 If the <u>Spelling and Grammar</u> window opens, use the options on the right, which correspond to the previous selections, to tell Word what you want to do with "problem" words. It will tell you when there are no more errors in the text.

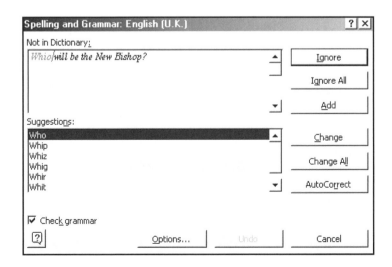

THE SPELLING AND GRAMMAR WINDOW
The various options in this dialog work as follows.

NOT IN DICTIONARY
The mis-spelled word is shown in this box in red.

SUGGESTIONS
If Word 2000 has one or more suggestions for an alternative spelling, it will put them here. Click on the one you need...

IGNORE
... or click here to ignore this particular instance of the word.

IGNORE ALL
Ignore All will tell the checker to pass all instances of the word.

ADD
Use this to add the word to your custom dictionary if you know it is correct – a name, for instance.

CHANGE
When you are happy with the proposed spelling, clicking this button will automatically replace the mis-spelled word with the one you have chosen from the suggested spelling list.

CHANGE ALL
This will change all the occurrences of the word in question to the selection throughout the document.

AUTOCORRECT
This button will make Word correct all the mis-spellings of this particular word that you might make in the future.

MANUAL CORRECTION
If you just want to make your own correction to the word, you can type the proper spelling for the word straight in the box, then hit Change. Word may ask you if you really want to do this if it does not recognize your manual correction.

1 Click on Options... in the Spelling & Grammar dialog box to personalize your spell checking functions.

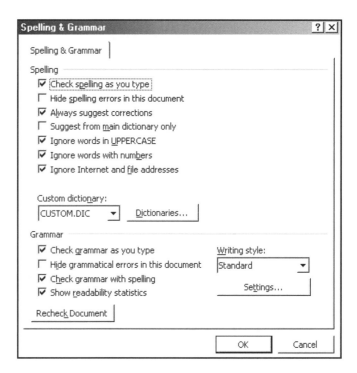

The spelling and grammar options dialog offers many ways of tailoring the functions to your personal needs.

CHECK SPELLING
Check or uncheck this to stop Word continuously checking your documents as you work through them.

HIDE SPELLING ERRORS...
If you don't like having red wavy lines turn them off by selecting this box. Do the same in the next box if you do not wish Word to suggest any alternative spellings.

SUGGEST FROM MAIN DICTIONARY ONLY...
If ticked, this option will not check for alternative spellings in your custom dictionaries.

IGNORE...
Tick these options if you don't need Word to spellcheck all of these items. Only do this if you are sure you don't need them.

You can create personal dictionaries of words to suit your needs, too. You may need different <u>custom dictionaries</u> for different users, or different projects. They are easy to use.

1 Select a custom dictionary from the list in the dropdown menu...

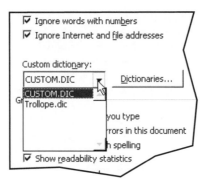

This box shows you the available custom dictionaries. Select the dictionary you wish to use (that is the dictionary into which your *new* words will be stored) from the dropdown list.

2 ... or create a new one by clicking <u>New...</u> from this window.

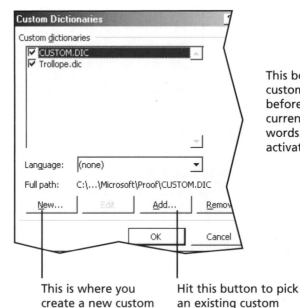

This box lists all the available custom dictionaries. No tick before them means they won't currently be searched for words. Tick the boxes to activate them.

This is where you create a new custom dictionary.

Hit this button to pick an existing custom dictionary.

WHY A CUSTOM DICTIONARY?

Custom dictionaries are useful when you have to check a document using technical language for instance, or when you are using specific words all the time (family names, martial arts terms, etc.) that will not be recognized by Word.

3 Choose a name for your new custom dictionary.

4 Type your filename in the box and hit Save. Your new custom dictionary will be activated.

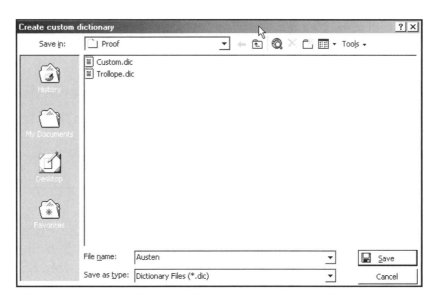

A NEW CUSTOM DICTIONARY

If you chose New, you will get the above window – listing all the custom dictionaries already created and available, so when you type in the name for your new dictionary, you do not choose a name that is already taken. Try to find a name that is relevant to the work at hand.

ADDING A CUSTOM DICTIONARY TO CHECK WORDS IN

Just follow the same process as with the New... button, but this time pick a custom dictionary from the list and hit Enter.

GRAMMAR CHECKING

As well as checking your document for spelling mistakes, Word 2000 will check it for grammatical errors. Inconsistencies will be underlined with green wavy lines. Press F7 to bring up the Spelling & Grammar window (see page 63) and grammatical errors will be highlighted in the same way as spelling mistakes.

SPELLING CARE

Beware of relying on the spell checker too much. No wavy lines in your text doesn't necessary mean it is error-free! "Form me to you" is correct as far as spelling is concerned, but doesn't mean anything and will not prompt any wavy lines.

1 After <u>F7</u>, click on Options... to bring up the <u>Spelling & Grammar</u> dialog box.

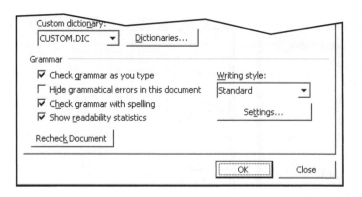

You can choose the style of your document and the grammatical rules Word will follow while checking it. Use the checkboxes to choose what Word will do for you. Select a <u>Writing style</u> from the list by clicking on the dropdown menu.

2 Click on <u>Settings...</u> to bring up the <u>Grammar Settings</u> box.

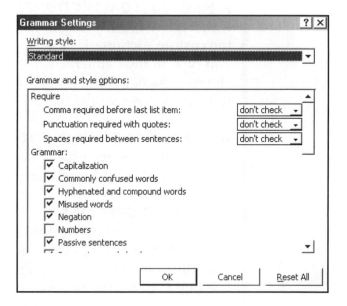

WRITING STYLES

This window shows the grammatical rules Word 2000 is currently using. You can select and deselect the ones you think are or are not relevant to your work. You can also go for a preset style from the <u>Writing style</u> box. Understanding grammar is very complex for a machine, so despite valiant efforts, the grammar checker is poor, and best avoided.

POINTS OF VIEW

4

Now that you have explored the basics of document creation with Word 2000, the time has come to explore some of the other key functions of the program. We'll look at printing your document, working with different views and using multiple windows. We'll also take a tour of the Microsoft Office Assistant and related help system, so that you can go about getting help if and when you need it.

DIFFERENT VIEWS

The default view method when you start Word 2000 is <u>Print View,</u> the mode that lets you use the new Click and Type function. There are other views to choose from though, depending on the type of work you're doing. Changing the way you look at your document isn't going to change its contents, but it is a useful way of adjusting your workplace so that you can work more effectively.

Normal View: For general editing. Nothing other than what you type will appear on the screen.

Outline view: To use when dealing with large documents.

1 Use the view icons at the bottom of the screen to switch between different views.

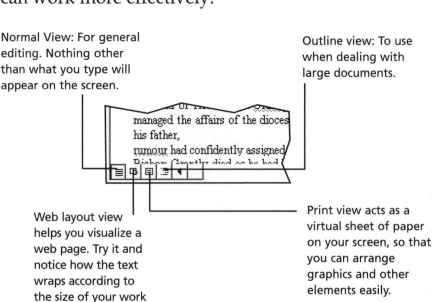

Web layout view helps you visualize a web page. Try it and notice how the text wraps according to the size of your work window.

Print view acts as a virtual sheet of paper on your screen, so that you can arrange graphics and other elements easily.

These various views can also be accessed via the <u>VIEW</u> menu in the menu bar.

MULTIPLE SELECTIONS

You can also view more than one document at a time, which is useful to compare one version of a piece of work with another, or cross-reference two different documents. To open more than one document at the same time, you can go through the open file operation once for each one, or you can actually open them all at once. To do so, hold down the <u>Ctrl</u> key as you make your <u>Open File</u> selections with the mouse. When you have chosen your files, hit <u>Return</u> and they will all open together. Because each Word document opens in its own separate window, and because they sit on top of one another, you won't see that all of your documents are there at the same time. If you have a look at the Windows taskbar at the bottom of your screen, you will notice that all the open documents are available from there. You can arrange your work windows so that one side of your screen contains one document and the other side another, or move them around in any other way to suit your convenience. Whatever you cut or copy in one of them you can paste in any other.

Each box has the title of the Word document it refers to on it. Click on one to activate the relevant document window.

NEW WINDOWS

It is also possible to view the same document twice, by creating a new window for it – useful when cutting and pasting in large documents. To do so, Select <u>WINDOW</u> in the main menu and then select <u>New Window</u>. Whatever modification you make to your document in one window will automatically be reflected in the other window.

   Some people prefer vertical lines to horizontal ones, so you might wish to split your document into two separate Word view panes arranged one on top of each other instead of creating a new window. The <u>Split View</u> option enables you to, amongst other things, edit the top part of your work while checking the content of the bottom part, or vice versa. This is accessed by selecting <u>WINDOW/SPLIT</u>.

1 Use the scroll bars to navigate each portion of your document.

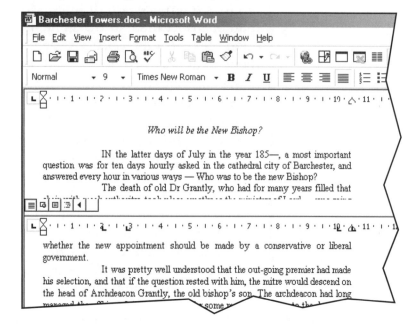

2 Click on the split line and drag it up or down to resize the areas according to your needs.

SPLITTING FEATURES
Once again, any modification made to one part of the document will instantly be made in the other part: after all, it is the same document you are working on. When you are done with your editing, you can go back to a single view by selecting <u>Remove Split</u> from the <u>WINDOW</u> menu bar.

MULTIPLE SAVING
If you have four documents open, do you really need to go through four save operations? Well, you can if you want, but the easiest way would be to choose <u>Save</u> from the main menu bar while holding down the <u>Shift</u> key. This will bring a new option in the save menu, <u>Save All</u>. If you click on it, all the documents that have been modified since their last save will be written to disk. <u>Close All</u> works the same way, again activated with the <u>Shift</u> key. If any document in a <u>Close All</u> procedure has been modified, Word will ask you if you are

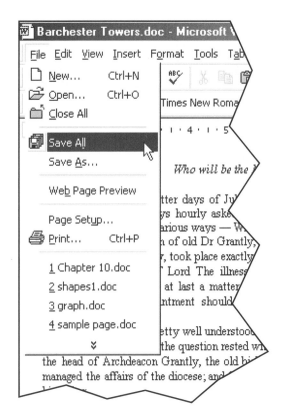

absolutely certain that you wish to close it without saving it first. One handy short-cut option only works for single documents, though. If you are done with a file, press Ctrl+W to close it quickly. If it is your last document, you will be left with the blank grey window that Word uses to indicate no documents are loaded.

If you are working with multiple documents, it might be useful to increase the resolution of your screen so that you have more room to view them all, instead of moving the mouse all the way down to the bottom of the screen to reach for the task bar where your documents are displayed.

HELP WHEN YOU NEED IT

If you are not sure about what a button or an icon does, simply sit your mouse pointer on it (without clicking) and wait a second. In most cases a little box will appear containing a brief description of what the item you're pointing at actually does.

PRINTING

The final stage of the production process for the majority of Word documents is the print process. While the paperless office may, in theory, make this step redundant at some point in the future, at the moment this is one of the most important steps.

The best place to start is to have a final look at what is actually going to be printed. Word, of course, has a function and toolbar icon dedicated to this particular task: the <u>Print Preview</u> button. Place your cursor at the beginning of your document and click this icon, or choose <u>FILE/PRINT PREVIEW</u> in the main menu bar.

1 Click on the <u>Print Preview</u> icon to start the printing process.

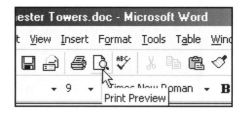

This is the toolbar you see in Print Preview mode.

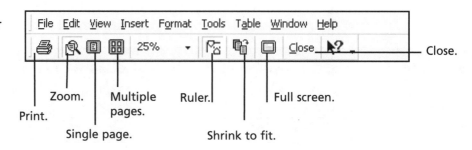

Print.

Zoom.

Single page.

Multiple pages.

Ruler.

Shrink to fit.

Full screen.

Close.

PRINT
You will use this button to print your document when ready.

SINGLE PAGE
If your document has more than one page, just one at a time will be displayed when you click here. To see the following or previous pages, you will have to use the scroll bar at the side.

MULTIPLE PAGES
This option will force Word to show your document more than one page at a time, depending on the layout you select.

ZOOM
Choose the level of magnification you need to view your work. You can either pick a value from the dropdown menu – the quick way – or type one into the box.

RULER
Lets you view or hide the ruler.

SHRINK TO FIT
If you click this icon, Word 2000 will attempt to shrink your document by one page by adjusting margins and page boundaries, to correct a small text overspill onto a new page.

FULL SCREEN
Click here to view your document in full screen mode. All the toolbars will disappear, so fortunately a box pops up to enable you to return to the normal <u>Print Preview</u> mode.

CLOSE
Returns you to the view mode you were in previously.

Note that in <u>Print Preview</u> mode, you cannot edit your text. All you can do is magnify or shrink a portion of your work by clicking the <u>Zoom</u> button to zoom in and clicking it again to zoom out. Any further changes you need to make to your document will have to be done in one of the other modes.

1 (Near image) Choose how many pages you want to preview at a time, and their layout, with this <u>Preview layout</u> menu.

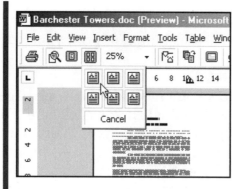

2 (Far image) Hit <u>Close</u> to return to normal <u>Print Preview</u> mode from <u>Full Screen</u> mode.

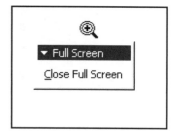

FINAL ADJUSTMENTS

If you selected a paragraph before entering <u>Print Preview</u> mode, its indentation can be adjusted by using the Ruler. To modify the whole of the document in <u>Print Preview</u>, return to normal view, press <u>Ctrl+A</u> to select all, and come back into <u>Print Preview</u>. If you are not satisfied with the way your document sits on the page, many aspects of the page layout can be adjusted from the <u>Page Setup</u> window, brought up by selecting <u>FILE/PAGE SETUP</u>.

1 The <u>Page Setup</u> dialog. The <u>Margins</u> tab is usually the first place to make adjustments from.

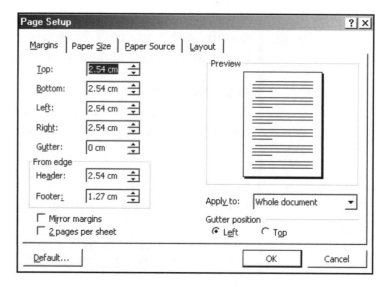

The tabs in the <u>Page Setup</u> dialog all have <u>Preview</u> panels so you can easily keep track of how your document is looking.

MARGINS

Your page margins can be adjusted here to increase or decrease the space on the page. The gutter is the space added to the margins to allow for binding. If you are printing a single page or loose-leaf document, you will not need any. If you need to produce left-hand and right-hand pages, like a book has, Mirrored margins will produce inside and outside margins rather than left and right. You can also use 2 pages per sheet to view a pair of pages – a **spread** – together.

2 Click the Paper Size tab.

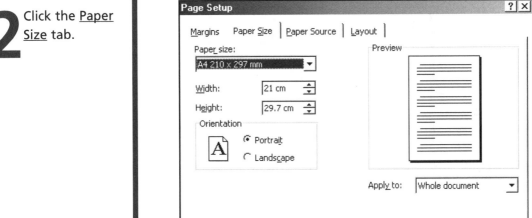

PAPER SIZE

You can alter the size of your page on screen with the Paper Size tab. Select a standard printer paper size from the drop down pick list, or enter a custom paper size into the Height and Width boxes. Be careful though – if you choose a page size larger than your printer can deal with, you may have difficulty when it comes to printing your document, confusing your printer or missing the edge off the text.

ORIENTATION

Select the orientation of your page here. The usual setting is Portrait (vertical). You may need to switch to Landscape (horizontal) to print notices or banners from time to time.

3 Adjust the <u>Paper Source</u> (near) and the <u>Layout</u> (far) tabs to match the printer and paper you have.

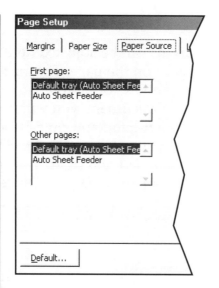

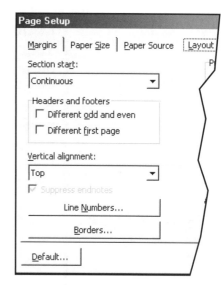

If you are not sure about an element in the <u>Paper Source</u> tab, you should refer to your printer's manual. This tab will be different for different printers, depending on their hardware setups. If you're not sure what you're doing here, don't worry; you shouldn't need to change these settings. The last pulldown menu in this tab gives you the chance to choose how your text will be lined up vertically: at the top of the page, centred, justified (equidistant from top and the bottom) or at the bottom.

4 Press <u>Ctrl+P</u> to get the <u>Print Setup</u> box.

PRINT IT
After one last preview, select <u>FILE/PRINT</u> in the main menu or press <u>Ctrl+P</u>. The <u>Print</u> dialog that appears on the screen can be a little daunting at first, but in most cases all you have to do is click on <u>OK</u>. The top frame contains the details of the printer Word is going to print to. If the printer listed is not the one you wish to

use, you can select another one – assuming you have a second one installed – from the dropdown menu. Clicking <u>Properties</u> will take you to the printer's set-up window. From this dialog box, you will be able to change your printer's settings. These are quite advanced, so unless you know what you are doing, you should not need to change them.

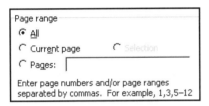
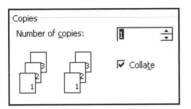
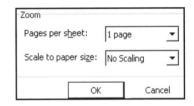

PAGE RANGE
You can choose to print everything, just the currently selected page, or to specify a range of pages, such as **1-4** or **2, 3, 6-10**.

COPIES
Select the number of copies of your document to print. A tick in the <u>Collate</u> box will print all the pages of your document in order and then start the second copy from page one. If you'd rather print all the copies of page one first, then all the copies of page two etc., then untick this box.

ZOOM
Here you can decide how many pages of your document will fit on a single piece of paper, and/or scale your document to fit on a particular paper type. The scaling of your document will be reset to normal when the printing is finished.

5 Once you have set up all your printing options, clicking the <u>Print</u> icon will use these as default and start printing your work straight away.

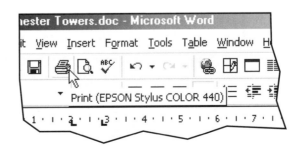

FINDING HELP IN WORD 2000

Help is readily available in Word 2000. It can be accessed in a variety of ways from every window you are working in. You will have noticed the Office Assistant, the animated paper clip sitting on your screen. Click it and type a question or a key word in the box at the bottom to get into Word's help files.

THE OFFICE ASSISTANT

This is the front line for getting help – unobtrusive and cute. You can move it around your screen by simply clicking it and dragging it to its new position. It will move out of the way by itself as you type anyway. It will activate as soon as you start typing inside it. Once you have typed in a question, you are taken to the help files proper. To make your search even easier, you can search these help files in three main ways: by a table of contents, with the answer wizard to answer a question, and by using a good old-fashioned index of terms.

What would you like to do?

- Troubleshoot printing
- Print a document
- Print property information or other document information

print

Options   Search

...I NEED SOMEBODY

The Office Assistant is only one of the ways to access the help files. Pressing the function key F1 is another, and selecting HELP/MICROSOFT WORD HELP is yet another.

1 This is the <u>Help by Content</u> window. Select a topic and sub-topics here to find the information you need.

Select what kind of search you are going to do: by content, with the wizard or using the index.

Click on a + sign to expand a topic into sub-topics.

An information sheet is shown by a "?" in a document box. It represents one sheet of help information.

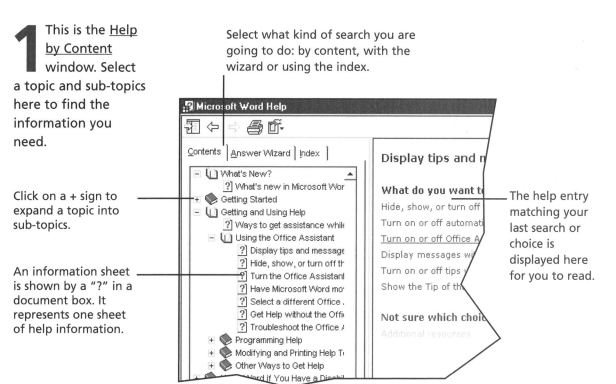

The help entry matching your last search or choice is displayed here for you to read.

The <u>Contents</u> tab works on the principle of organizing similar items together in categories and subcategories, a process known as nesting. Click on the plus sign in front of a book to be presented with a series of sub-topics. Repeat this process until you find the information sheet you need. If you make a mistake and follow the wrong track, clicking on the minus sign will collapse the whole topic so that you don't end up with scores of sub-topics confusing your search.

MORE HELP

Very often one help page will send you to another one for related information. If you are used to browsing the internet, you will have no problem whatsoever with this way of navigating help pages – just click on the coloured links. If additional resources are available for the item, the phrase <u>Additional Resources</u> will be displayed in colour and not greyed out. These are usually links to Microsoft internet sites where you can get up to date information.

The <u>Help Wizard</u> tab is the one you get to after typing a query in the Office Assistant, while the old fashioned index can be found throughout Windows 98 and is used by a great numbers of programs.

1 The help icons are there to help you navigate in your quest for help.

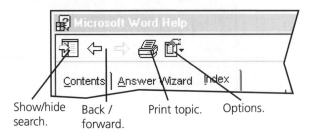

Show/hide search.   Back / forward.   Print topic.   Options.

SHOW/HIDE TAB
If you are working on a small screen, you can hide the search window by clicking here. Click on this icon once more to show it again.

BACK/FORWARD
These arrows will display the previous and next help pages you have already been to – in just the same way as working with an internet browser would.

PRINT
A help information sheet can be printed for future reference.

OPTIONS
This is the Options icon, which once again works like an internet browser.

You can choose a different Office Assistant by clicking it and then clicking on the <u>Options</u> button. In the <u>Gallery</u> tab, use <u>Previous</u> and <u>Next</u> and select the character you feel the most affinity with. There are up to eight to choose from. The <u>Options</u> tab in this dialog box will present you with a series of options to fine-tune the way the Office Assistant behaves.

Another kind of help is available to you, the <u>What's this?</u> buttons, accessed by either typing <u>Shift+F1</u>, or choosing <u>HELP/WHAT'S THIS?</u> from the menu bar and clicking on the item you want to know more about. Try it on text, buttons and menus and familiarize yourself with this very fast and effective way of getting help.

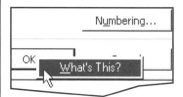

Right-clicking while placing the mouse pointer on a button or a feature brings up a little <u>What's This?</u> box. Click on it to get specific information about this particular button or other function.

If you hold the mouse still over a button or an icon for a second, Word 2000 will display a <u>Tool Tip</u> – a small yellow box with the icon's name in it so that you are sure to use the tool you need.

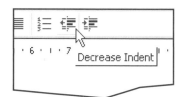

From time to time, you will find a <u>Show Me</u> button in the help pages themselves. If you click on it, you will get a short animation showing what you are trying to do. In the same vein, you will sometimes see a lightbulb pop up above your Office Assistant. Click on it and you will be offered extra information about the task at hand.

ONLINE HELP

The final type of help you can get is straight from Microsoft's web site. Select <u>HELP/OFFICE ON THE WEB</u> to be taken to a site dedicated to problem solving.

IT MOVES!

Check out Office Assistant from time to time: it's always on the move, coming to life as soon as you perform a task, be it when you print a document, perform a search or save your work. If a light bulb appears above it, clicking on it will give you more information about the function you are currently working with.

REPAIRING WORD

Word 2000 will look after itself. However, it may happen that some files useful for top performance of the Office 2000 package will be corrupted after a system crash. It is good idea to run a system check from time to time from within Word, just to be on the safe side. To do so, select <u>HELP/DETECT AND REPAIR</u> from the main menu bar. Word might need you to insert your Office 2000 CD into the drive to proceed.

1 <u>Detect and Repair</u> will help you clean up Word and make sure everything is in perfect order.

If your shortcut to Word has disappeared from your Windows' <u>Start</u> button, tick the <u>Restore my Shortcuts</u> box to put it back.

This optional repair system is also available for the whole Microsoft Office package. Insert your Office 2000 CD in the CD drive, and follow the instructions on screen.

2 You can also check the health of your Office 2000 setup as a whole.

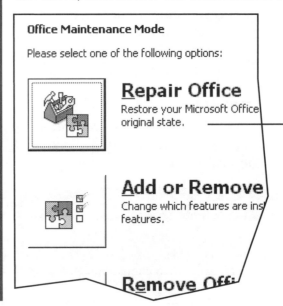

The Microsoft Office 2000 CD should autoload as soon as you insert it in the drive. Click on <u>Repair Office</u> and be prepared to wait a while for the check up to complete.

STYLES & FORMATS

5

To be clear, a report written by more than one person has to be consistent in its format and planning, otherwise the same information might be presented in as many ways as there are co-authors. To avoid this, Word 2000 provides you with styles that divide your work into sections, like chapters in a book. A master document can be created and sliced into separate files that you can distribute for editing.

FORMATTING TEXT

Styles are very useful for separating your text into a series of clear items, and for differentiating sections of your work. You can get a list of them by clicking on the <u>Style</u> box on your main toolbar – the one that usually reads "Normal". You'll get even more of them if you hold down the <u>Shift</u> key at the same time.

1 Click on the <u>Style</u> dropdown menu and choose the text style you need.

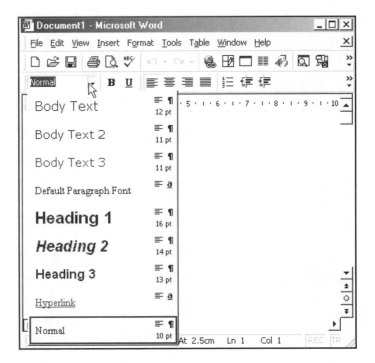

If you want to modify an existing style, you can do this from the <u>Style</u> dialog box, accessed by selecting <u>FORMAT/STYLE</u> from the main menu bar.

2 Change the styles by using the Style dialog box.

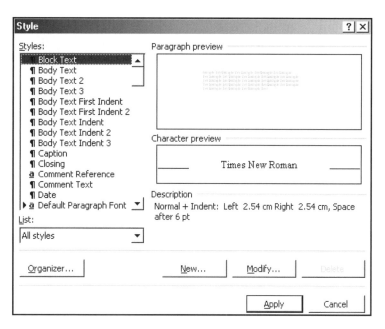

To modify an existing style, select it from the list and click Modify.... If the style you need doesn't appear in the list, select a different set using the List dropdown menu. All the styles will be previewed in the Paragraph and Character windows.

3 Create your own styles by clicking on Modify...

4 Name your new style by clicking in the box. You can add formatting and even give the style a shortcut key.

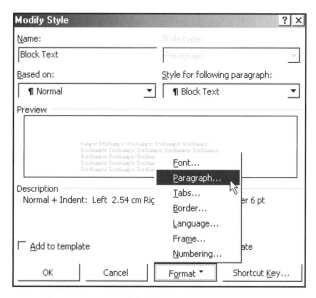

If there is a style you would like your new one to be similar to, select it with the Based on box before making changes.

Select the items you want to modify in the style you have chosen from the <u>Format</u> dropdown list. Each item in the list will bring up a new window to give you total control over the formatting of your styles. If you want Word 2000 to update all the occurrences of this style throughout your document, just tick the <u>Update</u> box. If you want your new style to be part of the template you are currently using, so it will always be available, select the <u>Add to template</u> box.

BRAND NEW STYLES

Styles can also be created from scratch. Instead of clicking on <u>Modify</u> in the <u>Style</u> dialog box, click on <u>New</u> to get the <u>New Style</u> dialog box. This looks just the same as the <u>Modify</u> dialog box.

1 Click on the <u>Indents and Spacing</u> tab to adjust your paragraph settings.

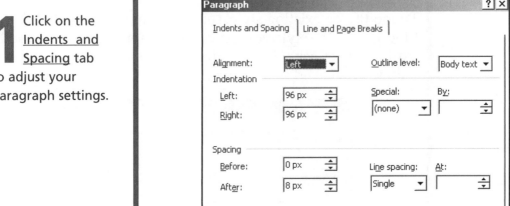

You can assign a specific indent, and change the paragraph alignment and line spacing. You can also change the outline level the style is going to act as in Outline View. There are up to nine outline levels to choose from. Select an outline level from the dropdown list. When you are satisfied with the new or modified style, hit <u>Apply</u> to activate it.

There is a quicker and less involved way of creating new styles for those who are not as fussed about paragraph formatting – select a style from the <u>Style</u> list, modify the font, size and basic formatting – Bold, Italic and Underline – as desired, then highlight the selected heading by clicking on it, type a new name and press Return. You have just created a new style, all without the use of any dialog boxes at all.

COPYING STYLES

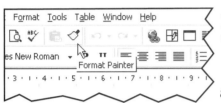

Copying and pasting works with styles too. Thanks to the Format Painter, you can assign a style to any paragraph in your document. It is a two-stage operation. First, select a piece of text whose format you wish to copy and click on the Format Painter icon. Then click and drag over the text you wish to assign that formatting to, and release.

The Format Painter icon.

MORE TO STYLES

Styles have a more advanced function than just making text look good though. They are also used to organize your work into headings, sub headings and text. To view the styles that has been applied to each separate paragraph, select TOOLS/ OPTIONS and open the View tab. In the Style area width, type a width, about one inch ideally. Your document is going to be split in two, with a new margin on the left of the size you allotted (this has no impact on the text itself) in which the styles applied to each paragraph are displayed.

1 Select or create a document with different styles applied to several close paragraphs to test the Style Name area, then assign a Style area width as described above and click OK. You'll see something much like the image to the right.

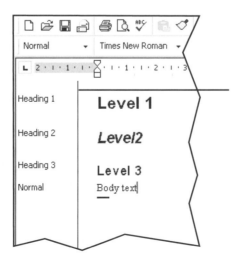

Drag this line to the left and right to adjust the amount of margin dedicated to displaying the styles.

2 Switch to outline view by selecting VIEW/OUTLINE from the FILE menu or from the icons at the bottom of the page.

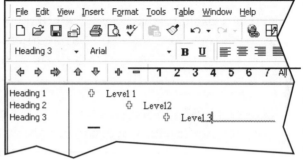

Double click on plus or minus to expand a level of outline to display the items of lesser levels it contains, like making an ordered number list.

When you modified or created a style in the Paragraph dialog box, you could assign an outline level. That outline level can be seen in action above – different outline levels are indented different amounts in the Outline View, indicating their respective priorities or importance. You can rearrange your work by dragging outline elements up or down and placing them under different headings. You can also see and vary this structure without entering Outline View. To do so, choose VIEW/DOCUMENT MAP in the main menu bar.

3 Use the plus and minus signs in the Outline View or Document map to navigate through your document by broad heading category and use the outline view to rearrange the different elements.

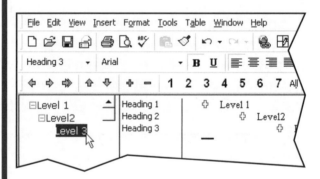

SUBDOCUMENTS

Now close the document map by selecting VIEW/ DOCUMENT MAP again. You are left in Outline mode with a series of headings. Your work can now be moved around or ordered in easily manageable small parts and subsections. You can even go one step further and create and save subdocuments. These bits of document can be easily distributed to various people who may not need an entire file. Also, because the outline is already prepared, if someone makes changes, the formatting will remain the same throughout the work and will not depend on anybody's formatting preferences. If everybody does their bit by following the same heading arrangements, the subdocuments will come back consistent and ordered. The document where everything is re-united – the one you have sliced up and scattered throughout the office – is called the **Master document**.

You will have noticed a new row of icons sitting at the top of your document when in <u>Outline</u> view:

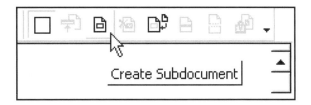

The most important icons are <u>Create Subdocument</u> and <u>Insert Subdocument</u>. You use these to create (and later re-insert) subdocuments for your master.

CREATING SUBDOCUMENTS

Click on a Heading and then on the <u>Create Subdocument</u> icon to set up a new page section. When all the subdocuments have been created, save your work. If you open the folder in which you saved it, you will see a series of new Word documents with their titles the same as the names of the various headings. These are the files that you should distribute to the relevant authors for editing.

Your main document is split into multiple subdocuments ready to be distributed.

C:\Joe's Folder						_ □ ×

File   Edit   View   Go   Favorites   Help

Back   Forward   Up   Map Drive   Disconnect   Cut

Address   C:\Joe's Folder

Joe's Folder

Joe.doc   Joe1.doc   Non vegetarian.doc   Sandwiches...

Vegetarian....

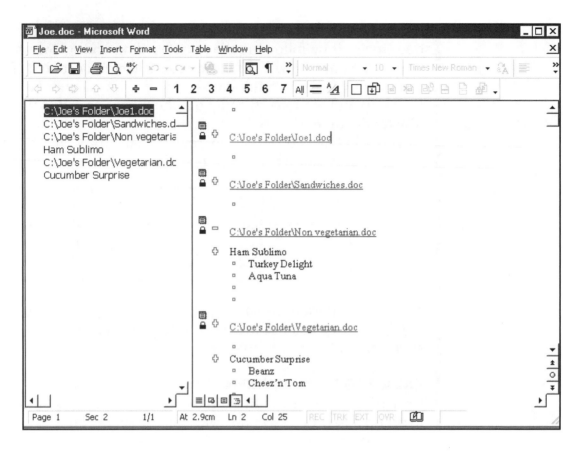

When you open the master document, all the subsections will have been replaced by paths – resembling web-style hyperlinks – that are the locations of its subdocuments. After

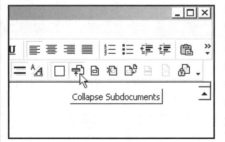

making sure that the files in the appropriate folder are the latest versions of your multiple authors' work, you can either click on the <u>Hyperlink</u> and open the subdocument in a new window, or click the <u>Expand Subdocument</u> icon and read the whole content in one window. If you choose to click on the hyperlink, the <u>Web</u> Toolbar will automatically appear. By using the <u>Document Map</u>, you can navigate the entire document one level at a time if you so wish.

HEADINGS AND THE WEB

Heading styles are extremely useful for creating web pages and Tables of Contents. Each heading can correspond to an entry in a Table of Contents. This Table of Contents can then be integrated into a web page, as well as being part of a final printed product. Here is an example of a web page that might be created from the example substructure on page 92.

1 Headings will help you quickly create a professional looking web page. For more on building Web Pages see page 150.

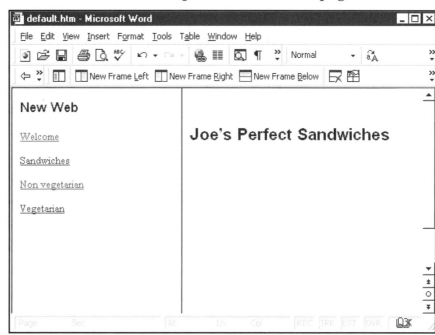

To use a Master document as the basis for a web design, you first need to convert all the subdocuments into HTML (Hyper-Text Mark-up Language) web-readable files. These can be done as a batch by selecting the <u>Batch Conversion Wizard</u> from the <u>FILE/NEW/OTHER DOCUMENT</u> submenu. Select <u>Convert from Word to another Format</u> in the wizard, and specify <u>HTML</u>. Select the folder where your subdocuments are gathered, and choose a different folder for them to be saved to. Your subdocuments will be saved as HTML files. Activate the <u>Web Page Wizard</u> (from <u>FILE/NEW/WEB PAGES</u>) and tell it where to find your new HTML files; it will be able to create a web site from the files you have just converted.

TABLES

The simplest way of creating a table is by using tab stops to subdivide information. The description of an item on the left, a bit of space, and a price on the right and there you go – a table. This section shows you how to put together a more formal version.

CONVERTING TEXT
Tables can be created easily from tabbed text.

1 Select the tabbed text that you want to turn into a table.

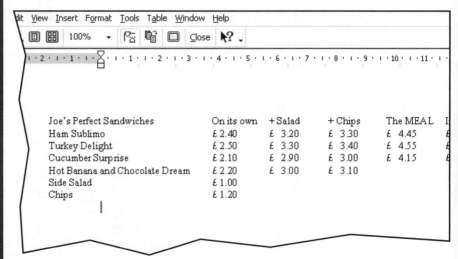

Tables offer several important options over tabbed text, such as easy item formatting, automatic borders for cells and for whole tables and, best of all, selecting text as a column. Highlight the text, then select the Convert option in the Tables menu. The Convert Text to Table dialog box will appear. The reverse operation is available to you too, and you can convert tables into text just as easily.

2 Use the Convert Text to Table dialog box to select the size of the table and to choose what character separates the entries. Click OK and your table will be created.

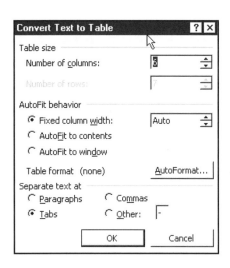

CREATING A NEW TABLE

Creating a table from scratch is as easy as creating it from formatted text. Clicking on the Insert Table icon on the main taskbar brings up a simple table size selection box.

1 Click on the Insert Table icon and drag the cursor until the table is the size you require, then click off.

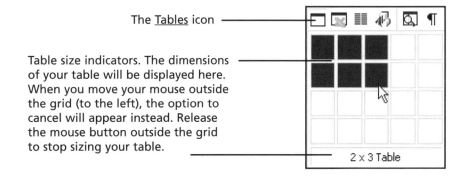

The Tables icon

Table size indicators. The dimensions of your table will be displayed here. When you move your mouse outside the grid (to the left), the option to cancel will appear instead. Release the mouse button outside the grid to stop sizing your table.

2 x 3 Table

First of all, you have to decide where the new table is going to go. The cursor's position will become the insertion point for your table. When you click on the Insert Table icon, a blank 5x4 grid will appear (the separate "boxes" in tables are referred to as "cells"). Move your mouse across and down to highlight cells until the table is big enough for your needs. Moving past the 5x4 limits will expand the blank grid indefinitely. When you have expanded the grid to the size that you want, click the mouse and it will appear in your work window at the cursor's position in your text.

Another way to design your table is through the <u>Tables and Borders</u> toolbar, activated by selecting <u>VIEW/TOOLBARS/ TABLES AND BORDERS</u>. The first step is to click on the <u>Draw Table</u> icon and then draw a rectangle that will contain the cells. Click once to start the rectangle and drag it to the appropriate size.

TABLES AND BORDERS – ICONS

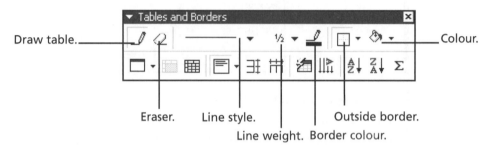

Draw table. Eraser. Line style. Line weight. Border colour. Outside border. Colour.

1 Click on the pencil icon in the <u>Tables and Borders</u> toolbar and start drawing your table. Start with the outline.

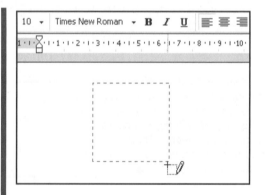

You might have trouble drawing vertical lines, but don't worry – Word will align your work properly.

2 When the outline is done, draw vertical and horizontal dividing lines for cells.

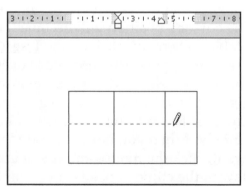

Each line in the table can have its own width, colour and style, set via the <u>Tables and Borders</u> toolbar. Select the line type to apply before drawing the line, or select one or more cells and apply the formatting to them.

ERASER

You can get rid of a line easily by selecting the Eraser tool and clicking on the sections of line to delete. Erasing the line between cells will merge them, while erasing the table boundary removes its formatting.

LINE STYLE

Lines can be styled by line type, thickness and colour with the Style, Weight and Color picklists. You can select the specific borders to apply the line to by clicking the Borders icon selection arrow. You can change any of the attributes for a line by selecting a new type of line, the colour, the strength and clicking on the line you want to modify. You can also change the fill of a particular cell by applying a shade to it. Simply click in the cell and pick a colour for it using the Shading Color icon. Changing a cell's borders will replace the formatting already in place for those lines that are affected. You can also choose the position of text in a cell with the Alignment and Change Text Direction buttons.

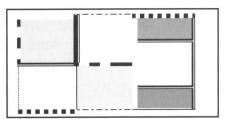

This is what can happen if you fill each cell in a different colour and make each line different.

ALIGNING COLUMNS AND ROWS

If your rows and columns are not of equal width and height, select the rows or columns that you want to spread evenly (it does not have to be the entire table) and click on Distribute Rows Evenly or Distribute Columns Evenly, as appropriate. The selected items will be balanced.

ROW/COLUMN SELECTION

To select a column or a row respectively, move your mouse pointer to the top of the column or the left of the row and click. You will know when you are in the correct position because the pointer will change into a fat black or white arrow.

TABLE INSERTION

You can also create a table from a dialog box without selecting any range of text or drawing the thing manually. Click in your document at the point you want to start a table and select Insert Table from the Table menu. The Insert Table dialog works as follows.

NUMBER COLUMNS AND ROWS

These boxes let you specify the numbers of rows and columns for your table.

AUTOFIT BEHAVIOUR

Selecting the Fixed Column Width button will force the table to be a specific width. If you select Auto, the table will be created using all available space between the left and right margins of your document. AutoFit to Contents will produce a table that resizes itself to match the text in its cells which, while often handy, can sometimes mean the table looks messy. AutoFit to Window forces the table to always be as wide as the page viewing window looking at it, which is extremely useful for designing material to go on a web page.

1 Using AutoFormat, select a format from the list in the box opposite.

AUTOFORMAT

Word has many different pre-set tables you can use. Clicking on AutoFormat brings up a list that you can scroll through, preview and select.

SET AS DEFAULT

This tells Word to base future tables on the current one.

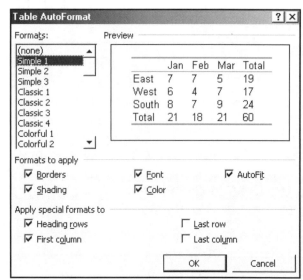

ADDING TO YOUR TABLE

Occasionally, after creating a table, you will find that you need to add more rows and/or columns. To do so, select a row in your table to add rows, or a column in your table to add columns. The icon immediately to the right of the Tables and Borders Icon on the main table will change from Insert Table to either Insert Row or Insert Column, depending on what you have selected. Click on it to add to your table.

You can obtain a more specific menu of table modification options (left) by selecting Insert from the Tables menu when your table is selected, or by right-clicking in your table. Selecting Delete from the Tables menu will conversely allow you to remove a selected section from your table.

SPLITTING AND MERGING CELLS

Any specific cell in a table can be split – that is, subdivided into two or more cells without changing the rest of the table. In fact, an entirely new table can even be created inside a cell, a process known as **nesting**. To split a cell, select it in the table and then choose Split Cells from the Tables menu. You'll be asked to specify a number of rows and columns to split the cell into; do so and click OK. You can insert a new table into the cell by selecting Insert Table instead of Split Cells.

The joining cells together is called merging. Select the cells to be merged, and then choose Merge Cells from the Tables menu. The cells will become one large collective cell.

1 To "nest" a table, just click in the cell you want a new table, and press TABLE/ INSERT TABLE.

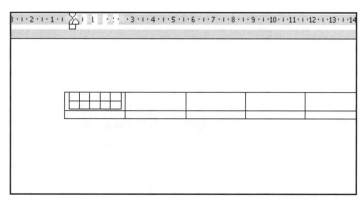

The small table at the top left is nested within the larger table.

USING TABLES

Tables can be used effectively to quickly and easily sort data, apply text formatting down a column rather than a row, and perform a number of calculations with **formulas**.

Joe's Perfect Sandwiches	On its own	With side salad	With chips	The MEAL	Inc VAT
Ham Sublimo	£ 2.40	£ 3.20	£ 3.30		
Turkey Delight	£ 2.50	£ 3.30	£ 3.40		
Cucumber Surprise	£ 2.10	£ 2.90	£ 3.00		
Hot Banana and Chocolate Dream	£ 2.20	£ 3.00	£ 3.10		
Side Salad	£ 1.00				
Chips	£ 1.20				

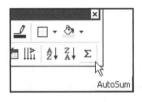

AutoSum

The AutoSum icon.

Formulas are instructions for Word to work out certain bits of information based on data in cells or different tables. If you are familar with Microsoft Excel, you will already know how MS Office formulas work. The most used formula is "sum", which adds values held in adjacent cells together. To perform a sum, click in a cell at the end of the row or column of data you want to add up and click the Autosum icon on the Tables and Borders toolbar. In the example below, the Autosum was performed in the last column and therefore calculated the sum of the whole row. To have a look at the way that Word has calculated the formula, type Alt+F9. Type Alt+F9 again to return to a simpler view.

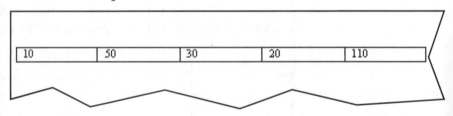

| 10 | 50 | 30 | 20 | 110 |

NAMING CELLS

The cells in a table each have a unique name, determined by how many columns from the leftmost they are (a letter) and how many rows from the top (a number). The first cell, at the top left, is A1. One cell to the right of this is B1. One cell below A1 will be A2, and so on.

FORMULAS AND CALCULATION

The fun begins when you start creating your own formulas, as in this example. In this case, the price of a sandwich and a side order amounts to the sum of the two items minus a reduction relevant to whether you get salad or chips (20 and 30 pence respectively). The Meal is the sum of the sandwich plus salad and chips minus 15%. The last column adds VAT at 17.5% to the meal price. The cells E5 and E6 are left blank because of the improbability of someone ordering both salad and chips with a banana sandwich...

Joe's Perfect Sandwiches	On its own	With side salad	With chips	The MEAL	Inc VAT
Ham Sublimo	£ 2.40	£ 3.20	£ 3.30	£ 3.91	£ 4.59
Turkey Delight	£ 2.50	£ 3.30	£ 3.40	£ 3.99	£ 4.68
Cucumber Surprise	£ 2.10	£ 2.90	£ 3.00	£ 3.65	£ 4.28
Hot Banana and Chocolate Dream	£ 2.20	£ 3.00	£ 3.10		
Side Salad	£ 1.00				
Chips	£ 1.20				

APPLYING A FORMULA

A cell can be manually assigned a formula, an advanced task.

1 To assign a formula to a cell, select the cell and then TABLES/FORMULA in the main menu bar.

Formula ? ✕

Formula:
=SUM(LEFT)

Number format:

Paste function: Paste bookmark:

OK   Cancel

If Word proposes a formula that you don't need in the Formula box, delete it. You can enter your own formula in this field instead (all formula lines start with =), or choose one from the selection provided in the Paste Function list. You can also choose a pre-set format for a cell value to be displayed in from a range of standardized accounting, date, time and currency formats by selecting one from the Number Format pick-list.

PASTE BOOKMARK

If you are working with information in more than one table, you can calculate formulas using values between the two tables by assigning a bookmark to each table you wish to use and ticking this box.

To create a bookmark for a table, or for any other object in Word 2000, choose <u>Bookmark</u> from the <u>Insert</u> menu and type a name for it. The name must start with a letter, but may subsequently contain numbers. It cannot contain any spaces, so the usual practice is to replace the gaps between words in the bookmark name with an underscore character, "_". If you type an unacceptable name, Word won't let you assign it to the object anyway, so you'll quickly work out if you're doing something wrong.

Most of the advanced table functions are beyond the scope of this book, but they are relatively self-explanatory once you've tinkered a little, and they receive extensive coverage in the Word 2000 help pages if you think you need to use them. It is worth bearing in mind though that if you really need to perform complicated calculations with tables, you are much better off using Microsoft Excel instead. Excel is another standard component of the Office 2000 suite of software packages, and will have come with your copy of Word.

SORTING TABLES

Word provides several powerful functions for helping you to sort data within a table. This is one of the most valuable uses of a data table, particularly if you need to work with a range of information types. Select the row or column to sort, and click on the <u>Sort Ascending</u> or <u>Sort Descending</u> icons to sort your entire table based on the area you've selected.

1 Use the two sort icons to quickly sort your table by ascending or descending values.

You can perform a more complex sort too – select your entire table by choosing <u>Select Table</u> from the <u>Tables</u> menu, then choose <u>Sort</u> from the same menu to open the <u>Sort</u> dialog:

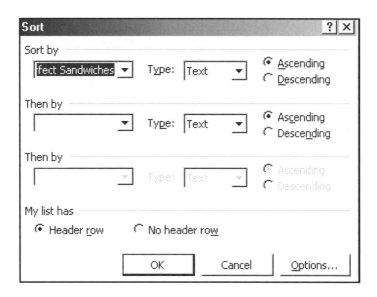

SORT BY... THEN BY...

Choose which columns to sort (<u>Sort By</u>) and then subsort (<u>Then By</u>) on from the dropdown pick lists. Specifying the <u>Type</u> tells Word what sort of data to sort – dates, numbers and text would all sort a date in the 11/12/00 format slightly differently. Selecting <u>Ascending</u> or <u>Descending</u> tells Word whether to go from A–Z and 1–9 or vice versa.

HEADER ROW

If you tell Word you have a <u>Header Row,</u> then the first row of the table will not be sorted; it will be left in place and used as the title of the columns in the <u>Sort By...</u> boxes.

SORTING SELECTIONS

If you select just a range of columns when sorting, they will be the only sort options in your <u>Sort By</u> boxes, but the whole table will be sorted. If you select a range of rows on the other hand, you will be able to <u>Sort By</u> all columns, but only the selected rows will be re-ordered. Either way it can be useful.

TABLE SHORTCUTS

If you have not selected an icon from the <u>Tables and Borders</u> dialog box when it is active – in other words when your table is ready to be adjusted, but you have not specified any particular task – an arrowed cross will appear in the top left corner of your table, and a small rectangle at the bottom right hand corner. You can click on the arrowed cross to drag and reposition the table in your document, and if necessary you can also use the cursor keys to finely adjust the position of your table. Clicking and dragging the small rectangle, by contrast, allows you to resize the table. This is quicker and easier than manually adjusting whole rows of cells and columns at the same time.

EASY RESIZING

It is however possible to resize each of the rows and columns in your table on an individual basis. Just position your pointer on the row or column line, click on it, and drag it around within the table. Let go of the mouse to stop dragging when the row or column has reached the size or position you wanted it to be in. If you make a mistake, you can of course just click <u>Undo</u> as per usual. If you want all the cells to be the same size, you can use the <u>Distribute rows evenly</u> and <u>Distribute columns evenly</u> buttons on the <u>Tables and Borders</u> toolbar as we discussed earlier.

TABLE NAVIGATION

You can get around your tables easily using key strokes if you want to use your mouse for other things – say interacting with a dialog box or options tab – or if you just want to save a bit of time if the table is getting big. The <u>tab</u> key is particularly useful. Use <u>tab</u> by itself to move forward one column of your table, and <u>tab</u> with the <u>Shift</u> key to move backwards on column. If you reach the last cell in the row, another column will automatically be created if you press <u>tab</u> again. You can also use the cursor keys on your keyboard to move around a table quickly, particularly Up and Down to move you one row higher or lower respectively.

PRINTING STATIONERY

6

In addition to printing your documents onto paper, Word also provides you with a wide range of support for printing onto other paper products, such as labels and envelopes. Getting a professional appearance to your correspondence can be very useful – but printing onto special stationery can be even more important if you need to send a lot of documents to many different people. Rather than go through and personalize every copy by hand, you can quickly and easily add personal details into a letter, envelope, label or other document from a list.

LABELS ETC.

In this section, we're going to look at the different types of paper product that you might want to print onto, and the ways that Microsoft Word can help. We'll have a look at the various types of envelope and label that are available to you, and how to print on them effectively.

THE ENVELOPES AND LABELS TOOL

Word's Envelopes and Labels tool works on the assumption that you are typing a letter, and that the first block of text at the top of your document is an address. It doesn't actually matter too much if this is not the case, as all the information it automatically grabs can be replaced, but for now we'll work on the assumption that you have written a letter from scratch, or used one of the templates from the Letters tab.

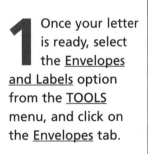
Once your letter is ready, select the Envelopes and Labels option from the TOOLS menu, and click on the Envelopes tab.

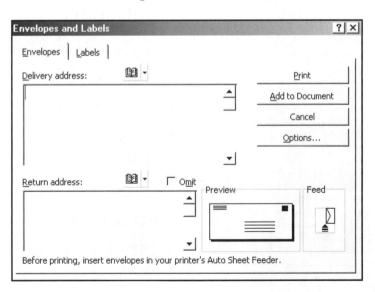

THE ENVELOPE DIALOG

Once the <u>Envelope</u> tab of the <u>Envelopes and Labels</u> dialog is active, you can change much of the information that it selects by default by entering the appropriate material into the various areas. The address that the letter is going to is put in the box labelled <u>Delivery Address</u>. If you had something highlighted in your document prior to opening this dialog box, whatever was selected now appears in this box, which can be useful if your letter is laid out in a non-standard format. If nothing was highlighted, then Word will look through your document until it finds something that looks like an address, or, failing that, take the text after the cursor or the first lines of text in the document. Your own address similarly goes in the <u>Return Address</u> box. If you have told Word your postal address in the <u>User Details</u> box (from the <u>Options</u> tab, which will be covered later), it will insert it here automatically for you. Otherwise, you'll have to enter it manually. If you click the <u>Omit</u> box, no return address will be printed.

The address book icons allow you to insert an entry from your contact book. The down arrow to the side provides you with a list of contacts available in your current contact book. Clicking on the icon proper opens the <u>Select Name</u> dialog box. Clicking on the <u>Add to Document</u> button inserts your chosen address straight into your document, in case you haven't already entered one. This button alters to <u>Change Document</u> if you already have an address in place that Word recognizes. The <u>Preview</u> box shows you roughly what the envelope layout will look like, and the <u>Feed</u> box tells you how to position your envelope to make sure it prints correctly on your current printer. Once everything is correct and the envelope is in place in your printer, click <u>Print</u> to print the envelope.

ADDING ADDRESSES

When you create a new contact, its details are automatically added to your current address book. The easiest way is to use Outlook, part of the Office 2000 package.

ENVELOPE OPTIONS

Clicking on the Options button of the Envelopes and Labels dialog – or clicking on the Preview window – will call up the Envelope Options dialog box. From within this section, you can modify your envelope to suit your needs.

2 Select the Envelope Size dropdown picklist to select the correct details of the physical envelope that you are going to print onto.

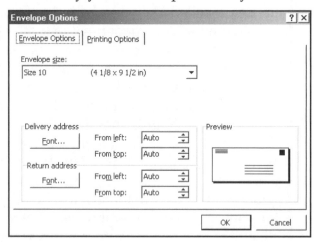

The Envelope size list should contain all of the different standard envelope types that you are likely to encounter. However, if your envelope is not listed, select the Custom Size type and enter the correct dimensions. The Font buttons will let you independently select fonts to apply to the destination and return addresses, and you can alter the position of the addresses with the buttons to the right of the Font button.

3 If the envelope did not come out as you expected, modifying the selections on the Printing tab of the Options dialog should rectify the problem.

By default, Word 2000 should give you the correct orientation and feed method to print your envelopes successfully. If these didn't work, check the print settings. You may be set up to print to the wrong type of printer, for example.

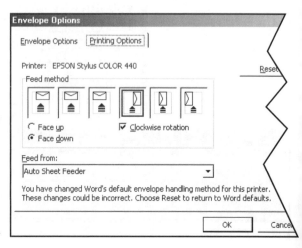

THE ADDRESS BOOK

You can use the Microsoft Address Book to provide you with addresses for your letters, as mentioned earlier. This function works with other Microsoft products too, so you can make use of your Outlook or Outlook Express address books, or obtain your mailing addresses from other similar sources.

1 Browse the Contacts dropdown list to select where you actually want to get your names from, then select a name in the list. Click on the Property button for a complete description of the entry.

Selecting New on the Address Book dialog opens the New Personal Address Properties box. This is where you can create a new address book entry. This will be stored for future use, and can be made available to a number of Microsoft applications for your further use, such as Outlook Express. Fill in the details required by clicking on each box that you want to enter information in, for each tab. You do not have to enter any more information than you want to, although for the purposes of printing an envelope you will need to enter a name and address at the very least. Some information is passed on from tab to tab. When you have put in all the required information, click OK.

Fill in your contact details to use with Word, Outlook Express and other programs.

LABELS

In addition to the various envelope functions that we've been looking at, Word can also print onto almost any of the many and various mailing labels for you. Select the <u>Envelopes and Labels</u> option from the <u>TOOLS</u> menu, and click on the <u>Labels</u> tab. This tab is laid out in a similar manner to the <u>Envelopes</u> tab, and the common boxes that the two tabs share work in exactly the same ways. If you completed the Envelope tab

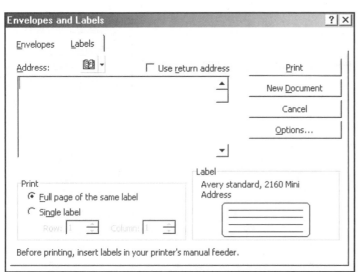

(page 106), the address you entered will be displayed automatically. If you entered a return address previously in the Envelope tab, you can reuse it in the Labels tab by ticking the <u>Use return address</u> button.

Click on the <u>Print</u> button to select how many labels you need to print – from a single one to a whole sheet of them.

Clicking on the <u>New document</u> icon will create a new Word document, called Label 1 by default. If you are going to want sheets of the same label in the future, you can save and re-use this document each time you want to print more labels, provided that the information and addresses that it holds are still current.

As with the <u>Envelopes</u> tab, Word will try to work out the correct address for your label. If it gets the details wrong, you can re-type the address in the <u>Destination Address</u> box, or select one from the address book as previously described. If you want to print a sheet with a different address for each label, then that is covered under Mail Merge, on page 112.

LABELS OPTIONS

Telling Word which type of label you are using is simple if you are using labels from one of the major brands that Microsoft knows about. If your labels are a standard type, simply select that type and Word will make sure your information fits the label and prints onto it properly.

Label Options

Printer information

○ Dot matrix

● Laser and ink jet   Tray: | Default tray (Auto Sheet Feed ▼)

OK
Cancel
Details...
New Label...
Delete

Label products: | Avery standard ▼

Product number:

| 2160 Mini - Address |
| 2162 Mini - Address |
| 2163 Mini - Shipping |
| 2164 - Shipping |
| 2180 Mini - File Folder |
| 2181 Mini - File Folder |
| 2186 Mini - Diskette |

Label information

Type: Address
Height: 2.54 cm
Width: 6.67 cm
Page size: Mini (4 ¼ x 5 in)

The labels that you can buy come designed either for laser printers – in standard sheets – or for dot-matrix printers, in fan-fold strips. You can select which category of labels you want to print to from the <u>Tray</u> option.

The most common brands of label are listed by their product serial number. Check which number of label you want to print to, and select it. If the labels you are using are not listed in Word, you can pass all the necessary details to the program by selecting the <u>New</u> button. The <u>New Custom...</u> label type dialog will appear. The top window shows you the approximate layout of your custom label. Each different measurement name is demonstrated here too, to make it easy for you to enter the correct information. Use this or enter the label's measurements in the fields below.

1 You will have to give your new label a name. Make sure that the name will help you remember the actual labels you are using.

New Custom laser

Preview

Side margins
Top margin
Vertical pitch
Width
Height
Number down
Number across

Label name: |

Top margin: | 1.27 cm   Label height: | 2.54 cm
Side margin: | 2.06 cm   Label width: | 6.67 cm
Vertical pitch: | 2.54 cm   Number across: | 1
Horizontal pitch: | 6.67 cm   Number down: | 4

Page size: | Mini (4 ¼ x 5 in) ▼

OK   Cancel

# MAIL MERGE

When you need to send the same document to a number of different people, you do not want to have to re-write the whole thing for each person. This can be avoided by mail merging. Mail merging means merging a letter with a database (a collection of data). Certain fields in your letter are left blank when you build it and will be replaced by elements in the database when the letter is printed. So you need two things: a specially designed letter and a database. The database can be created from scratch or come from an existing one, such as your Outlook contact book.

SETTING UP

In order to set up a mail merge you need two key elements: a letter and a data source. The letter will be your "master document" – what you will send out to people – and the "data source" is where you store the information that you will put into your master document. When you write your letter you leave blanks ("fields") which will be filled by the information in your data source. When you have prepared your letter and created your data source, you merge the two together into one document which you will print out, page by page, or send in another way (email for example). Word guides you through all of the stages step-by-step.

The <u>Mail Merge Helper</u> has three buttons that divide the mail merge into three stages. The initial box enables you to set up your mail merge with a minimum of fuss. You can use any previously created letter or template as your main document, or you can create a new one specifically for this mail merge.

1 Create or open the document you want to personalize for your list of people and call up the Mail Merge Helper by clicking on TOOLS/ MAIL MERGE in the main menu bar. This will be the Main Document.

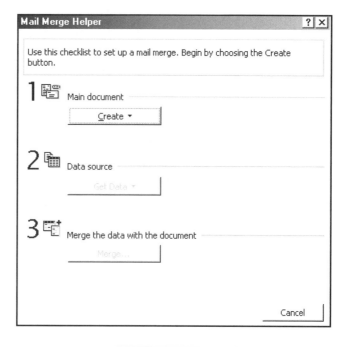

2 Click on step 1: Create and select Form Letters to create a merged letter.

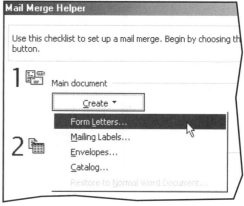

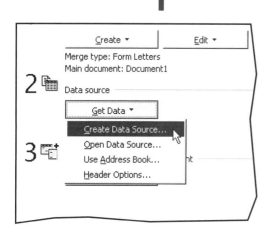

3 Click on step 2: Get Data and select Create Data Source to create a new source for your data, or Open Data Source to use a ready database like an Excel file or a .csv list. Word will create a new document for you, this will be the Data Source for your mail merge.

When you click on an item in the <u>Create</u> list for the first time, Word asks you if you wish to use the open document (the one you were in when you clicked on <u>Create</u>) as your main document, or if you wish to create a new one to use. If you do not have one prepared, start a new one, otherwise select the <u>Active Document</u> option to use the current one. Your <u>Main Document</u> will be the one that Word uses to add its data to. It is the document that is sent out to people when you've added their details. When you have created your document, another button appears in the <u>Mail Merge Helper</u> – the <u>Edit</u> button. This allows you to edit your main document.

STEP TWO

The second step of the process is to specify where the data you need to merge in your main document is. This will be the name and addressing information mentioned above. Click on the <u>Get Data</u> button to do this. You have the choice of using an existing Data Source from database applications such as Microsoft Excel and Access. Address Book has its own option if you would like to import from this program. The data source used in your letter's header might not be the same as the data source for the letter itself: it may have been created in a different program. If you need to create a new data source, you'll be asked to define headings that you will be entering data for.

4 If you did not specify a database file already prepared, you will need to create your data source. Select the "Fields" in this box that reflect the information to go into your document.

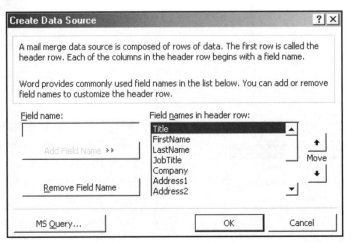

A data source is like a table. The data (the personal and work details about the addressees) will be contained in rows and columns. Each column has a name, called a field name. The information in your data source will contain field names that you will be selecting to go into your Word document. Each row is a new record, and that record's fields will go into the main document as specified, one record at a time. Word offers certain default field names for you when you need to create a new data source. If the right fields aren't there for you, you can easily add new ones by typing in the Field name and clicking Add Field Name. Note that the field name is just for your reference, and has no actual effect. You can sort the order of each field name in the data source by using the up and down arrows. This too makes no difference to the merge. When you click OK, you will be asked to save this data source. The same place as the Main Document is recommended.

5 Add data to your data source, field by field.

Data Form		? X
Title:		OK
FirstName:		Add New
LastName:		
JobTitle:		Delete
Company:		Restore
Address1:		
Address2:		Find...
City:		View Source
State:		
Record: ◀◀ ◀ 1 ▶ ▶▶		

ADD YOUR DATA

The data source you just saved will be empty, and will look like the one above. Click on the Edit button to create a series of entries in your data source, one by one. These will be the details you need to merge. You won't need to do this if you imported a data source. When you add to your data source, you will notice that all the fields you had in the Create Data Source dialog box list are present in this window. Type your information in the relevant boxes, and click Add New at the end of a record to start a new one. You can leave some fields blank, but remember that if you do, nothing will be merged when you use this particular field.

THE DATA FORM BOX

Field names are the same as those set up in the <u>Create Data Source</u> dialog box. This time though, instead of changing the field names, you can enter your information as you want it to appear in the various fields in the finished mail merge. Add new contacts by clicking on <u>Add new</u>, and if you make a mistake, press <u>Restore</u> to bring back the original record. You can navigate through your records by using the left and right arrows. The double arrows will jump ten records forwards or back from the current one. If you "lose" a record and need to find it, or if you think you've duplicated one, click on <u>Find</u> to search for records. You may want to have a look at the whole setup, including all of the records that you have created – for example if you aren't sure you have been filling one of the fields in correctly – if so, click <u>Source</u> to do this. You will see all of the fields at the top and all of the information that you have entered below it in rows. You can modify any information you like this way. When it is finished, you will be asked to <u>Edit Main Document</u> if it contains no merge fields.

MAIL MERGE TOOLBAR

Now that you have a master document and you have your datafile, you need to go about adjusting the master document to incorporate the data. The process of integrating this data into your letter is known as inserting merge fields. A series of icons on the <u>Mail Merge Toolbar</u>, which appears automatically when you edit your master document, will make things easier

INSERT MERGE FIELD

Locate the position on your master document where you want a field to be entered, click on it, and select <u>Insert Merge Field</u> from the toolbar. Pick the correct data field from the dropdown list, and it will be entered into the document. Repeat this process until all the changing data you want to incorporate is positioned in the correct spot. If you need to change the fields available or the data they contain, you can click on the <u>Mail Merge Helper</u> icon to return to the dialogue box, or click on the <u>Edit Data Source</u> to modify your records.

VIEW ENTRY

You can also click on the <u>View Entry</u> icon to see the actual data merged in position within your document. This will show you what the letter will look like with the contents of the first record in your data source put in place. You can scroll through all of the entries in your data source one by one if you wish, by using the arrows to the right of the <u>View Entry</u> icon.

6 Check that your merged document will be correct by seeing what it will look like with each record, using the arrows on the <u>Mail Merge Toolbar</u>.

Dear «FirstName»

We finally agreed on a date for the meeting. It will be held in London on the 25th August at 10.45. You will get full details as soon as they are available.

Yours truly,

Bob, «JobTitle»

Insert Merge Field ▾   Insert Word Field ▾   ABC |◀ ◀   1   ▶ ▶| Merge

MERGE

Click the <u>Merge</u> button to carry out your merge when it is set up. You have to place at least one Merge Field to select this.

7 Check that everything works, and click on Merge.

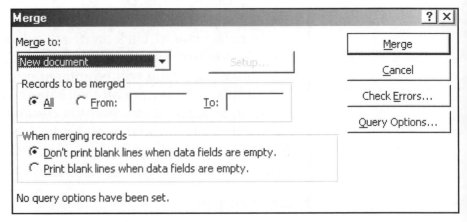

Before applying the merge, it is a good idea to check that everything is working as planned. Select the <u>View Merged Data</u> icon, and browse through your records one by one to check for discrepancies. If everything looks good to you, and the data you want is being put in place, click <u>Merge</u>.
You don't have to merge all of the records you have in your data source if you don't want to. You may want to leave some out, or do them later. The <u>Merge</u> dialog box helps you to fine tune your sorting and your final output. <u>Merge</u> can be accessed through the <u>Merge</u> icon in the <u>Merge Toolbar</u> or through the <u>TOOLS/MAIL MERGE</u> menu entry.

MERGE TO
This tells Word what to do with your merged document. You can store it as a new document, send it straight to the printer, or send it via email. If you select the latter, a <u>Setup</u> button will activate (see below). In general, it is better to store your merge as a new document so that if anything goes wrong with the printing, such as using the wrong paper, you do not have to re-generate the merge. You can also store it for future use if appropriate too. <u>Records to be merged</u> selects the records you wish to use for the merge – useful for very long databases – and <u>Check Errors</u> makes sure everything is working OK.

GENERATING THE MERGE

The Query Options allow you to set a range of selection filters that will allow you to specify types of records that will be processed. When you are happy with everything in the Merge dialog box, click <u>Merge</u>. If you are generating a Merge to a Word document, each page will be separated by a page break, so that you can just print the entire output to your regular printer. If you chose to send the mail merge direct to your printer, you will need to look for your results in the printer's paper tray. If you chose to email your merge however, you still have a bit more to do via the <u>Merge To Setup</u> window, which will pop up if you merge to email.

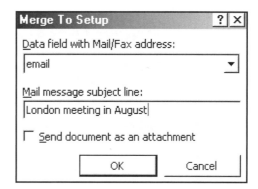

You need to set up your email merge by completing the boxes in the dialog box shown above.

DATA FIELD...

Choose the name of the merge field that contains the email address. It is usually "Email_Address". You will need to make sure that you filled in this field in each record of your data.

SUBJECT

Type in the subject of your email in this box.

ATTACHMENT

If you wish to send this letter as an attachment, tick here. An attachment will send your letter as a file that the addressees can store, open and/or retrieve.

ADVANCED MAIL MERGING

There is a whole lot more that you can do with a mail merge, but there is simply not enough room to go into it in detail here. Most advanced mail merging functions involve sorting your mail merge fields in a variety of ways. One very useful feature of Word's mail merging is the possibility to edit each letter according to certain criteria. For instance, you can send the same letter to people in Great Britain and in France regarding a video conference to be held at a particular time on a given day. This would be problem-free if France and Great Britain were in the same time zone, but they are not. Therefore you would need to check the addressees' country of residence and change the time printed accordingly.

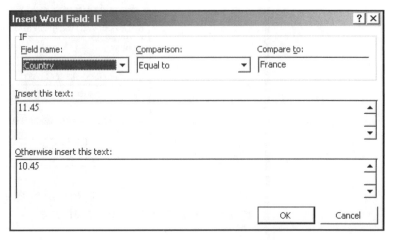

The box above shows how you change the text printed according to the <u>IF</u> function. If certain criteria are met in certain fields, then certain instructions will be carried out. To access this from the <u>Mail Merge Toolbar</u>, select <u>Insert Word Field</u> and then <u>IF</u>. In the example above, if Word finds the word "France" in the "Country" field of the data source, it will insert the text "11.45". In all other cases, Word will insert "10.45". For the specific above example, you would have to make sure that there were no other countries in your data source. If there were, however, you could swiftly tailor the above <u>IF</u> statement to take this into account.

ADDING GRAPHICS

7

Bring some colour to your work and give your imagination the free rein it deserves by exploring the ways Word 2000 handles graphics, boxes, lines, captions, colours, shapes, images of all sorts – even film clips and sounds! Let your text float and add speech bubbles and balloons... Seriously, once you start playing around with graphics, you will see that they are not just for fun – they can be a great way to enhance a document or to emphasize a point.

LINE ART AND TEXT BOXES

Line art is the most basic part of the Word graphic engine, and uses a line, a box and a sphere. The line art shapes are accessed by clicking the relevant icons on the <u>Drawing</u> toolbar, at the bottom of your work window. If this toolbar is not visible, select <u>VIEW/TOOLBARS/DRAWING</u>.

Pointer.   Free rotate.

THE DRAWING TOOLBAR

All of Word's graphic functions can be accessed through the <u>Drawing</u> toolbar. Several of the advanced options are accessible through the <u>Draw</u> menu on the left, but the key icons at the moment are going to be the <u>Pointer</u>, which you will use to select drawing objects, and the Line Art tools, the four icons to the right of the <u>AutoShapes</u> button – straight line, arrow, rectangle and oval respectively. <u>AutoShapes</u> are pre-made polygons, lines and boxes that come in a wide array of shapes and functions, and Word actually classes the Line Art items as <u>AutoShapes</u> too, but they'll remain the key building blocks of your graphical work. The other icons on the toolbar include line style and shape fill options, 3D effects, and the ability to insert various other objects.

Click on the line, the arrow and the double arrows, the box, or the circle to draw your first piece of line art in Word. Click somewhere on your page and drag the image to roughly the desired line or shape, and then release the mouse button. Hold down the <u>Ctrl</u> key while drawing to treat the point you clicked on as the center not the corner, and the <u>Shift</u> key to draw a perfect square or circle. Once you release the mouse button, you can resize your image by selecting the shape, moving the pointer to one of the sizing handles and dragging to the desired size. If you hold down the <u>Shift</u> key while you do this, the object will keep its original proportions. To select an object, click on the <u>Pointer</u> and then click on the object. You can also move your mouse over an object and see if a double arrow cross appears. If it does, click to select the object.

If you draw more than one shape, you may end up with the shapes on top of each other. The order the shapes are displayed in may not be the one you need.

1 Draw the three shapes as in the diagram (right).

This collection of shapes was drawn in this order: rectangle, oval, circle.

2 To change the order of the shapes select one, click on the <u>Draw</u> button and choose <u>Order</u>. Tell Word to bring the item forwards (or to the front) compared to other objects, or to send it backwards.

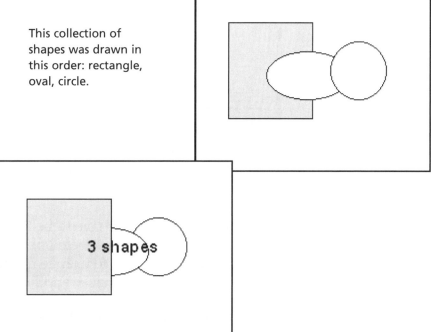

3 shapes

In the example on the previous page, the order of the shapes has changed so that now the rectangle is in front of the oval, the circle is behind the oval and they all are behind the text, which was not visible before. The order-changing options can also be accessed from the popup menu when you right-click on one of the objects. If you find placing your shapes difficult you can invoke an invisible grid that your objects will "snap" to, making placement a lot easier – all your shapes will be automatically aligned.

1 Turn the grid on through the Drawing grid button on the Drawing toolbar.

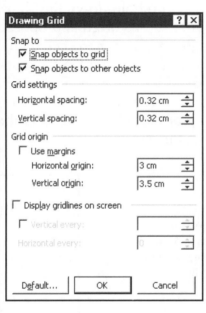

USING THE GRID

You have a high level of control over your grid. You can arrange your objects easily by snapping them to the grid or to each another, set the interval between each vertical and horizontal line, select Margins for a grid based on your work, specify the grid's origin points, and show the grid on screen if you think you need to see it. Note that the grid is for your reference only – it will never be printed. When you are drawing and need to fine tune the position of the shape that you have drawn, use the Nudge buttons, which you can find in the Draw menu. These will move your shape up, down, left or right one place on the grid.

ADDING COLOUR

Your objects do not all have to be the same colour. Click on the pot of paint to fill a selected object with the colour displayed. If you want to change the colour, click on the down arrow to its side and choose another from the list.

The same principle applies to the line fill. You can modify the type of line by clicking the Dash Style or Line Style buttons on the Drawing toolbar. The button after it will let you add arrowheads to lines. If you right-click on an object and select <u>Format AutoShape</u>, you will get a dialog box that will present you with a lot of options to fine tune your shapes. Most of the options available to you should be familiar from other, similar formatting options boxes.

EFFECTS

Word 2000 lets you add 3D and shadow effects to your objects as well. Click on the <u>Shadows</u> and <u>3D</u> buttons to get a number of shadow and 3D options for your selected shape, then click on one to apply it. Note that you can't have both a shadow and a 3D effect on the same object at the same time. Also you will no longer be able to assign colour or formatting to the object's lines because the lines will have effectively disappeared.

1 To select multiple objects, <u>Shift</u>-click them. Then right-click and choose <u>Group</u>.

GROUPING

Sometimes you will need to move items around without changing the relative positions, or modify more than one item at the same time. You could of course alter each drawing object separately, but that's rather time-consuming and you will often find that it is difficult to get them back into the same relative alignments. Instead, you can transform a selection of objects into a group and move or alter the whole group together. Select the objects to group and click <u>Group</u> from the <u>Draw</u> menu or the right-click selection picklist.

2 Do your modifications. Word will remember that you grouped an object and when you right-click on it again it will give you the choice to <u>Regroup</u> it again. Fill options and line formatting work in group mode too.

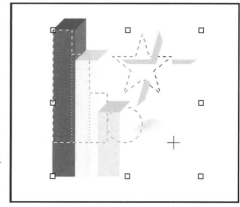

ADDING TEXT AND AUTOSHAPES

You can also add text to your shapes. All you have to do is right-click on one of your shapes and select <u>Add Text</u>. A text box matching the dimensions of your object will appear. Type your text in and change the font as you wish. There are many more shapes available to you than the basic line-art shapes, though. You can have stars, banners, geometric shapes, arrows and much more via the <u>AutoShapes</u> button.

1 Click on the AutoShapes button to get a wider array of shapes.

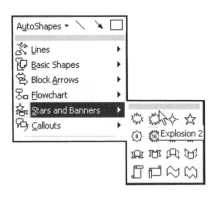

You can do anything you could do with basic shapes i.e. rotate, resize, scale, fill, line fill with AutoShapes. Some, such as the Callouts, come with text boxes already built in automatically.

Use the diamond-shaped formatting points that some shapes have to resize different aspects of them.

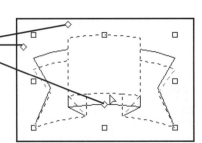

TEXT WITH SHAPES

When you place an object over some text (see page 127), you can decide how the object will interact with it using either the <u>Picture</u> toolbar or the <u>Format AutoShape</u> option, accessible by right-clicking in the object. You can choose from a number of preset options to flow the text around your shape (called **Wrapping**) or have the two mingle. It is easy to tune the way text wraps around an object. From the <u>Picture</u> toolbar (not <u>Drawing</u>!) click on the <u>Text Wrapping</u> icon. Choose <u>Edit Wrap Points</u>. Your object will be surrounded by a red dotted line with handles, similar to the resizing ones. Move these squares around to expand or contract the text wrapping.

1 Click on the <u>Text</u> <u>Wrapping</u> icon and choose <u>Edit</u> <u>Wrap Points</u>.

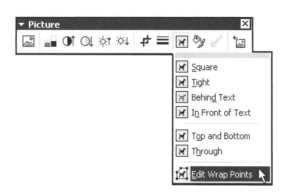

2 Click and hold points to drag them to the desired position. This will control how close to a picture your text will be.

NEED MORE POINTS?

If you find that you don't have enough wrapping control points around the picture, you can add more by clicking on the red dotted line.

DRAWING OBJECTS AND WORDART

Adding pictures to improve the look of your documents, or to illustrate examples, doesn't stop here. WordArt offers you even more possibilities to add more to your documents by creating and editing stunning textual illustrations.

1 Click on the <u>WordArt</u> icon on the <u>Drawing</u> toolbar.

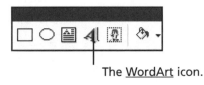

The <u>WordArt</u> icon.

2 Choose the basic style of <u>WordArt</u> you want by clicking on one of the preview styles.

WordArt Gallery

Select a <u>W</u>ordArt style:

OK   Cancel

3 Input your text, and change the font, the size and the basic formatting. Click on OK when you are happy with what's written. Your WordArt text is inserted as an object.

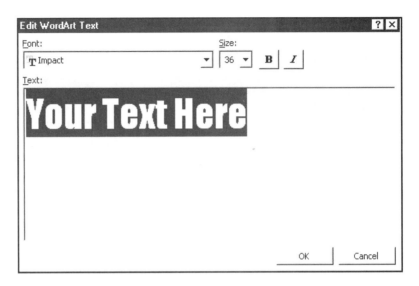

4 If you aren't happy with your text, or you would like to add more, just double-click on the existing text to alter any of the settings, including the basic WordArt style.

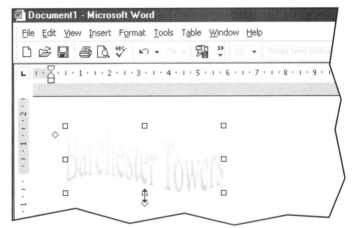

USE THE HANDLES

You can modify the look of a piece of WordArt by dragging the various handles that are placed around it. If you are not happy with the text itself, double-click on it to go back to the Edit Word Text dialog box. More options are accessible from the WordArt toolbar that pops up automatically when you select a WordArt object, including aligning the text differently and rotating the overall WordArt shape. The various toolbar functions are as follows:

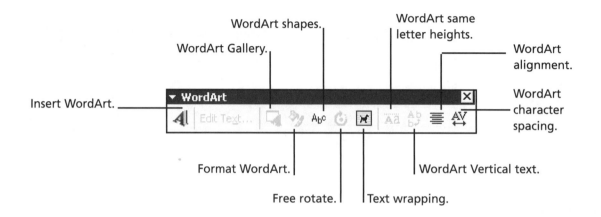

INSERT WORDART
Click on the Insert Wordart button to start a new WordArt.

FORMAT WORDART
Existing WordArt can be modified through the Format WordArt button.

WORDART SHAPES
A shape can be applied to the WordArt from the picklist Shape gallery via the WordArt Shapes button.

FREE ROTATE
The WordArt object can be freely rotated through 360 degrees by dragging a handle activated through this button.

WORDART SAME LETTER HEIGHTS
The Same Letter Heights button will force WordArt to make each letter the same height, whether it is a capital or not.

WORDART VERTICAL TEXT
Use this icon to toggle between vertical and horizontal text.

WORDART CHARACTER SPACING
The Character Spacing icon lets you select how far away the characters will be from each another.

1 Each piece of WordArt can be tweaked further by using the <u>Format WordArt</u> icon (or by selecting Format/WordArt in the main menu).

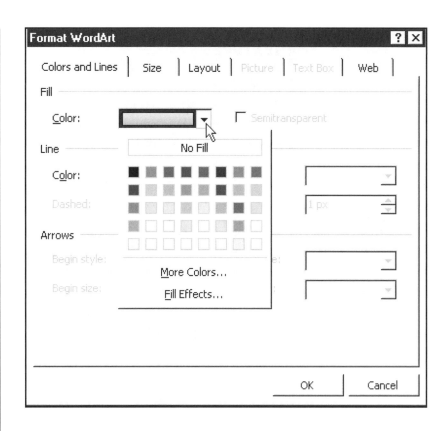

2 Select a colour for the face of your WordArt. If the offered choices are not enough, click <u>More Colors</u>.

3 Select <u>Fill Effects...</u> from the colour menu to select a texture for your selected piece of WordArt from the dialog box.

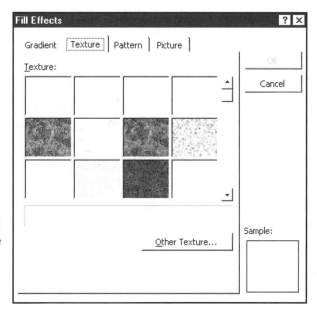

The <u>Fill Effects</u> dialog box is well worth exploring. You can choose how many colours your object will have or apply a texture to it.

TEXTURES

A texture is a special type of image that is seamless, which means that when you repeat it to cover the whole of your image, you can't see any borders where it joins the next copy of the image. It is ideal for web backgrounds as well as for WordArt and AutoShapes. Word 2000 offers you a wide range of textures to play with, but you can also import your own if you have any. Seamless textures are available for free on the web (see page 188).

To select a texture, be it marble, stone, wood, fabric or anything else, just click on the one you want. You can import all sorts of image files to act as new textures as well, as long as the format is supported by Word. New textures might not be as seamless as Microsoft's official ones, though.

WORKING WITH PICTURES

It is just as easy to insert a picture to use as a texture for your WordArt. Click the <u>Picture</u> tab of the <u>Fill Effects</u> dialog (see page 131) and select one. Unlike a texture, pictures will be stretched across the face of your object and not tiled.

You can also insert pictures straight into your document by selecting <u>INSERT/PICTURE</u> from the main menu bar or through the <u>Picture</u> icon on the <u>Picture</u> toolbar. The picture will be inserted at your current cursor position, but you can drag it anywhere, add a border or check the wrapping as if it the selection was a text box or an AutoShape.

If you need to adjust your picture (it could be too dark, too dull or too big, for example) the icons on the <u>Picture</u> toolbar will provide the options that you need. First of all, select the picture you want to work on by clicking on it. Use <u>VIEW/ TOOLBAR/PICTURE</u> to call up the <u>Picture</u> toolbar:

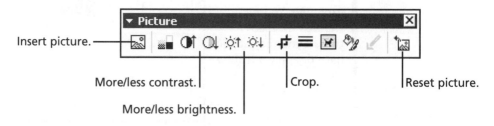

Insert picture.

More/less contrast.

More/less brightness.

Crop.

Reset picture.

CONTRAST AND BRIGHTNESS

Increase or decrease contrast or brightness. You can use these as much as you need to get the right balance.

CROP

If your picture is too big, or contains elements you don't need, you can crop it – focus on just a small section – by clicking this icon then selecting the area to display. This will not resize or stretch the picture, just hide the bit outside the crop box.

RESET PICTURE

This is a special <u>Undo</u> button for pictures. Click on it to restore the picture to the way it was when you imported it.

If you do not have any pictures handy on your hard drive, you can either scan one directly into your document or use <u>Clip art</u>. Word 2000 has an extensive array of this, accessible through the <u>INSERT/PICTURE/CLIP ART</u> entry in the main menu bar. Clip art is available for free from the web or you can buy reasonably-priced CDs full of it.

1 Import Word's own clip art to your documents by selecting <u>INSERT/ PICTURE/ CLIP ART</u>. There's a whole gallery to choose from. Double-click on a category to view the pictures inside, or on a picture itself to import it.

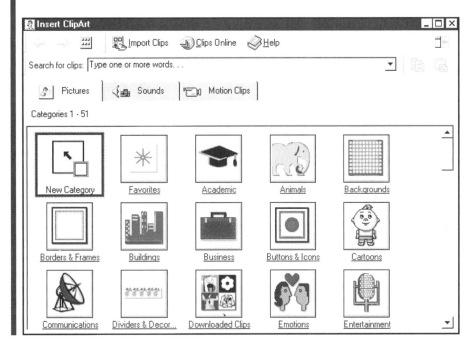

SELECTING CLIP ART

With the <u>Insert Clip Art</u> dialog box open, click on one of the small images to open the category. If the clip art you are after is not there, click on <u>Keep looking</u>. Use the back and forward arrows to work your way through the gallery – it's a bit like using a web page. You can also use the <u>Search</u> box to browse the gallery using keywords. Just type the search words in this box. You can import your own collection of clip art using the <u>Import Clips</u> button, or grab some from Microsoft's site on the internet by clicking the <u>Clips Online</u> button. In order to access clip art, make sure that you have set Word up to do so. The clip art gallery stays behind your current document once you have chosen an item unless you actively shut it, making inserting and editing faster and easier.

Below is an example of clip art with a Callout AutoShape. It is a good idea to <u>Group</u> composite images like this to make sure that when you move one part, the other moves with it. This is exactly the same as grouping line art or AutoShapes.

1 Add a callout speech bubble to your clip art by choosing one from the <u>Drawing</u> toolbar <u>AutoShape</u> button. Move the callout to where you want it. You can adjust the speech bubble's size and the direction of the pointer. Click in the Callout and type to add text. Edit the text in the callout as any other text.

Another way to add extra information to an illustration or object is to use a caption. The caption will be linked to the object for ease of reference, so that Word can automatically name all the illustrations in a document. To add a caption to an image, select the image and choose <u>INSERT/CAPTION</u> from the main menu bar. Change the name label to relate it to the image in question and click <u>OK</u>.

Caption dialog box:

Caption:
> Figure 1

Options
Label: Figure | New Label...
Position: Below selected item | Delete Label
Numbering...
AutoCaption... | OK | Cancel

AutoCaption dialog box:

Add caption when inserting:
- Microsoft Excel Worksheet
- Microsoft Graph 2000 Chart
- Microsoft Map
- Microsoft PowerPoint Presentation
- Microsoft PowerPoint Slide
- Microsoft Word Document
- Microsoft Word Picture
- Microsoft Word Table

Options
Use label: Figure | New Label...
Position: Below item | Numbering...
OK | Cancel

1 Use the AutoCaption box to customize how the caption will describe your object type. You can use this for all sorts of objects, not just images – just choose from the list.

From the <u>Caption</u> dialog box (shown above), select the style of the automatic numbering that Word assigns this – and the other captions – in your document. It can be 1, 2, 3 or i, ii, iii or a, b, c etc. Word will add a numbered caption every time you add an object to your document if you click on <u>AutoCaption...</u> and check the relevant boxes. This is very useful if your document mixes a lot of images in with its text. You can also select the type of object you want a caption to be automatically associated with, so it doesn't have to be an image. Each option (label, numbering) can be re-done for each type of object.

RELATIVE POSITIONING

One last point about the placement of your object. You can lock your object (image, table, WordArt, etc.) to the paragraph it was imported into, so that when the paragraph moves up or down, the object moves with it. To do this, open the <u>Format Object</u> dialog box by right-clicking on the object and choosing <u>Advanced Layout</u> in the <u>Layout</u> tab.

1 Lock your image to text by checking the <u>Lock anchor</u> box in the <u>Advanced Layout</u> tab.

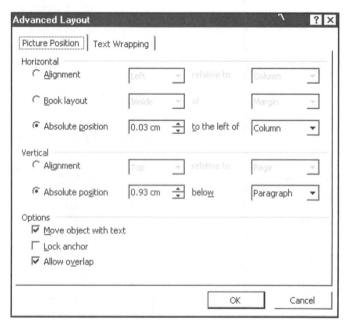

An anchor can be a paragraph, a line or a character that the object is relative to. To see the anchor of an object, go to <u>TOOLS/OPTIONS/VIEW</u> and tick the <u>Object Anchors</u> box.

PRESENTING INFORMATION

Another object you can may want to add to make your work clearer is a chart. Word 2000 has a specific tool for adding charts, based on Excel. Select <u>INSERT/PICTURE/CHART</u> in the main menu. When you click on this menu, Word will open a new document – a datasheet – that you use to put data in to so that you can set up a chart. You fill in your data, and your chart is generated from it. You can fully customize the chart that you have created.

1 Use the Datasheet (bottom of picture) to create a chart. Begin with a blank data sheet, which will appear when you select INSERT/PICTURE/ CHART from the main menu.

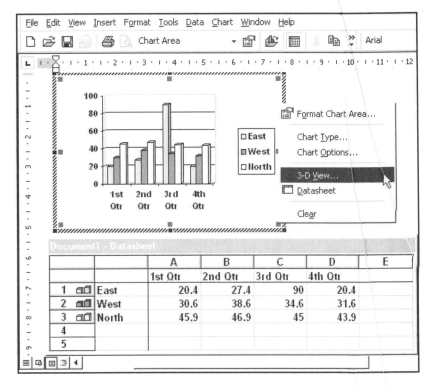

Modify the datasheet to suit your needs and specify what your chart will look like by clicking on the menus (brought up by a right-click), from Chart Type..., 3-D View..., and Chart Options... All of the elements in your chart can also be configured via a right-click on the chart itself or from the various icons on the Chart toolbar.

Format chart area.   Import file.

FORMAT CHART AREA
Select an area in your data and format it by clicking here.

IMPORT FILE
You can import existing datasheets from external programs such as Excel 2000 and create Word charts with them.

IMPORTED OBJECTS

Word 2000 let you place a range of other files into your documents. Provided you have a copy of the program that created them, you can even edit them, via an advanced tool called OLE. An "object" can be any file that is external to Word. Select INSERT/OBJECT from the main menu.

Use the Object dialog box when you want to insert a new object into your Word document. Call this box up by selecting Insert/Object.

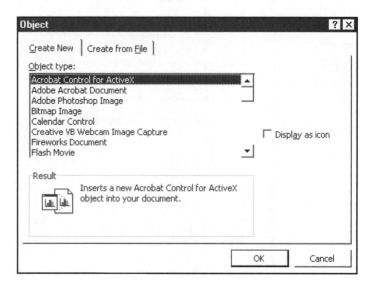

CREATING AN OBJECT

First, you need to select the object type you want to insert into your document from the list of file types in the main box. Click on one to see a description in the Result box. You can choose to create a new object in the application concerned, or import a file that was created previously. If you select Display As Icon, the object will be linked through from your document, but will only appear as a standard document icon of that type. If you do not select it, the document will appear roughly as it would if it were opened in its appropriate application. Either way, double-click on it to open it fully.

In order to create a new document, you need to have an application – a program – that deals with that particular object. Select the Bitmap object, for instance, and Microsoft Paint will open a small window in Word. If you draw something in the Paintwork window you will notice that Word's toolbars have disappeared and have been replaced by

Paint's. When you are satisfied with your piece of work, click outside the Paint work window to be taken back to Word. Microsoft Paint will disappear to the background, leaving only the art you just created as an object in your Word file. If you right-click on the object and select Edit, you will be taken back to Paint. The same principle is applied to other objects. If you wish to import an object you have previously created, choose the Create from File tab from the Object dialog box:

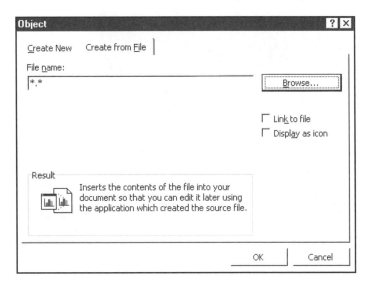

BROWSE...
Select your object using this button. Go through your files until you find the one you need.

LINK TO FILE
Every time you – or somebody else – modifies the original object, an updated version of it will appear in your document if you tick this box. If you don't, you might end up displaying an outdated version of the file if the original has been updated since you inserted it.

DISPLAY AS ICON
This works in the same way that its counterpart on the Create New tab does.

RUNNING AN OBJECT

In order to "run" an object, that is, to activate a non-Word document such as a movie or sound clip, you need a program that is capable of reading it. Therefore, if you distribute documents with objects in them, you need to make sure that the person at the other end will be able to view them. To run the object, simply double-click on it.

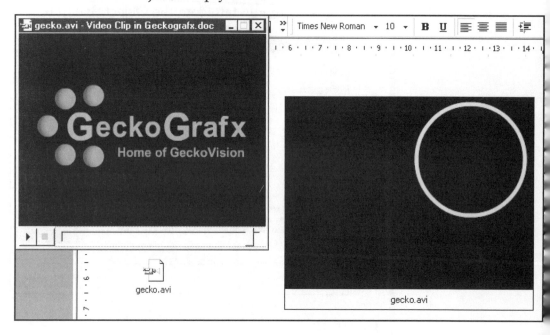

MOVIES

Using a movie clip as an example, if the object is not displayed as an icon, it will show the first frame of the film only and it will play in your document where it is placed when you run it. If the movie is in your document as an icon, it will play in a separate window when you double-click on it.

There is one thing you should be aware of: unlike images, objects created by other programs that you insert in your documents are not embedded. This means that they are not saved with the document. If the location of the file the object refers to changes on your hard drive, or if it is deleted, the object in your document will not work, and Word will ask you for the location of the file.

SHARING DATA

Using Word, it is possible to interact with other Office 2000 programs and share your Excel database with your accountant, or your PowerPoint slides with your designer. Exchanging information – copying the latest chart, result or report – can be done with any of your colleagues. Word 2000 also enables you to send your document via email straight away, or browse the internet in search of additional information or pictures – and it can even design web pages.

SHARING DATA AND PROGRAMS

You have learned how to import objects from other applications. You know that virtually anything can be cut and pasted into your Word 2000 document, and edited from within it. Now we are going to insert data from other Office 2000 programs as a "link", so that any modification to the linked object will be reflected in your Word document. This is particularly useful when sharing databases, charts and other files that keep on changing.

To start a link, leave Word temporarily and copy the data you wish to insert in its home application (Excel, for example). Do this by selecting Copy from the application's file menu once

1 Select the type of file you want to paste your data as. Activate the Paste Link radio button if you want this data to be updated in your Word document as it is updated in the source application.

you have selected the object you want to copy. Go back to your
Word document, position the cursor where you want the data
to be pasted into your text, and choose EDIT/PASTE SPECIAL
from the main menu bar. Using the options in the Paste Special
dialog box, select the correct application for your work. You
can just Paste the object, which will remain static – as it is – in
your document, or you can select Paste Link, which will
include a link from Word to the object that you have just
pasted. When you select this option, if the object changes (if

This shows you where
your link comes from.

Use the radio buttons to
decide the type of
update you would like.

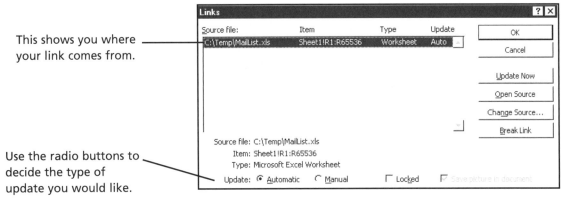

new sales figures are inserted in an Excel sheet for example),
Word will automatically update the object in your document to
reflect the changes.

When the object has been inserted with a link, you can
change the status of the link in various ways. You can set the
link to update automatically or manually, for example. Use the
Links dialog box to activate changes. This is accessed through
the FILE menu when the linked object is highlighted. The
information at the top of the dialog box shows you what the
source address of your link is – this is where the object is
stored. This also tells you what sort of object it is (an Excel
worksheet in the example above). Using the buttons to the side
of the box, you can Update Now to update the link, Open
Source to open the program that the linked object was
generated with, Change Source... to specify a new object to
link to (another file), or you can also break the link, making the
object a standard one as described above. If you break the link,
the object will no longer be updated.

HYPERLINKS

Another way to link to information from an external program into Word is to use the <u>Paste as Hyperlink</u> option, also available from <u>EDIT</u> in the main menu bar. This will create a Web-style hyperlink to a source document which will open automatically, along with its source application, when you click on it. You can also Hyperlink to a site on the internet or intranet, or to a specific file or a part of a file in any of those places. You can create a simple hyperlink to another Word document on your hard drive as well.

If you want to paste a hyperlink, you do not need to copy the whole of a document to create the link. All you have to do is select (for example) one cell in Microsoft Excel, copy it, go back to Word 2000 and choose <u>Paste as Hyperlink</u> from the <u>File</u> menu. Then, when you click on the hyperlink in your Word document, it will take you to that cell in the Excel document. If Excel is not open, the hyperlink will open it for you. You can also start a hyperlink from Word by typing in some text and creating a hyperlink for a particular file from within Word 2000. Select the text and right-click on it. In the dropdown menu, choose <u>Hyperlink</u>. For more on hyperlinks, see page 155.

1 An example of interactivity between PowerPoint and Word 2000. PowerPoint is "sending" a file direct to Word. All of the formatting will be retained.

INTERACTIVITY

Word 2000 is part of the Office 2000 suite. This also contains Excel 2000, PowerPoint 2000 and Access 2000. Because all the programs belong to the same package, they can all communicate with one another. You can specifically export and import documents between all of the programs, by using the <u>Send to</u> option from the <u>FILE</u> menu in Word.

Paste your Microsoft PowerPoint 2000 slides directly into Word.

ONLINE DISCUSSION

Word 2000 allows you to place your documents on the internet for online discussion. With an online discussion you and as many other people as you wish can discuss a document that you have "posted" on the internet. Everyone involved can see the document in question at the same time, and make comments. Each comment will be placed in a separate window at the bottom of the screen, while the document being discussed will appear at the top. This is very a powerful feature that lets you discuss your documents on a global basis. The comments that you or others make can be made in real time (if everyone is connected at the same time) or stored as messages to come back to later. You can choose to be notified when a comment has been made or when somebody has replied to a comment of yours. Going into the technicalities of online discussion is beyond the scope of this book as it is one of the very advanced features of Word 2000. You should contact your Network Manager or your Internet Service Provider if you wish to use this feature. You will also probably need to install the Microsoft Office Server Extensions to set up your own online discussion. To access an online discussion, click on TOOLS/ONLINE COLLABORATION/WEB DISCUSSIONS and follow the instructions on the screen.

Your Network Manager or Internet Service Provider should be able to help you when setting up an online discussion.

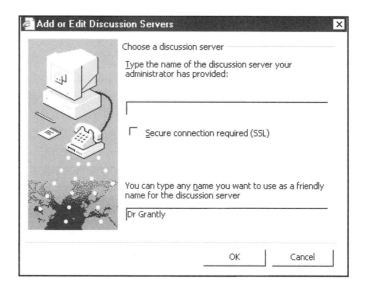

SENDING EMAIL FROM WORD

Any document written in Word 2000 can be sent as an email from within Word itself. This handy feature makes communication while you are working a lot simpler. When you select the email option, Word transforms into a fully-fledged email program, with all the standard email options such as forwarding, attachments and the like.

To send a document via email, choose Send to from the FILE menu. You will get a series of options in the menu as shown below. You will only need one of the top two options.

1 The most common options are the Send To Mail Recipient and Send... (as Attachment) options. Access these from the FILE menu's Send To options.

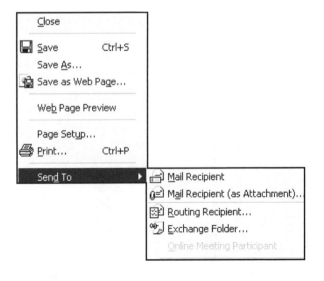

Select either of these options and Word will change into an email editor. You can still edit and modify your text in any way you like at this stage, but you will now find the <u>Email</u> toolbar sitting on top of your work window.

2 From the <u>Sending mail</u> dialog box, change your message if you need to, and add the addresses you want to send it to, then just click <u>Send</u>. Your message will go to your regular emailer's outbox.

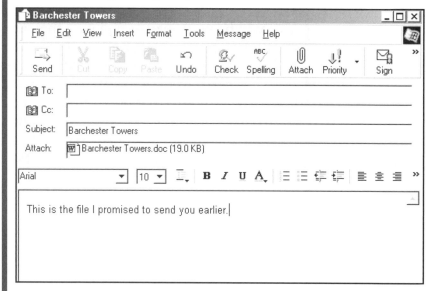

Use the options to operate the emailer as you would most standard email programs. Fill in your recipients and add attachments using the following tools:

ADDRESS BOOK
Click on this to open your own address book to select recipients.

PRIORITY
Setting levels of priority to your messages will enable others to sort your emails by order of importance.

EMAIL OR ATTACHMENT?

Select <u>Send to Recipient</u> if you want to send your document as a letter. The raw text of your document will appear in the email message itself. If you'd rather your addressee was able to save, open and edit this document from within Word, send it as an attachment – the text will not appear in the email message at all, but will consist of a Word file sent along with an explanatory message.

ATTACH
If you need to send a file along with your message, click on this button and browse to select the relevant file(s).

TO
This will be your main recipient – the person to whom the message is primarily addressed. Type their email address in this box or use your address book (the book icon). You can send Carbon Copies (CC) of the mail to people as well, if you want to notify them of information without actually involving them in the discussion. You can also Blind Carbon Copy (BCC) your message to people – if someone receives a BCC, those who were sent or CC'ed will not know about the BCC person receiving a copy of the mail.

SEND
Once all the information has been entered, hit the <u>Send</u> button to send your email. This will put your message in the Outbox folder of your current email editor (e.g. Microsoft Outlook). The Outbox folder contains all messages that you have written and that need sending. Depending on your email setup, you may have to open your email program and then send your message manually, or Word may send the message itself.

If you chose to send your document as an attachment, you will be presented with a different, separate window – the <u>Send Mail</u> window – that works basically the same way as the one shown page 147. This window will be part of the current email program on your computer. Office 2000 comes with its own dedicated email program (Outlook) though and this will, for most people,

TO, CC, BCC

You can send the same document to more than one recipient in the <u>To</u> box: simply separate each email address with a comma. The person or people that you sent the message <u>To</u> will be able to automatically reply to all the other recipients. Those that you have <u>Cc</u>'ed or BCC'ed will automatically just reply to you and not to everyone in the list. If you have only one main recipient and some Carbon Copies, the reply from your main recipient will not reach all the other people the original message was sent to.

be the email program that opens automatically. If yours is different, just treat it as if you were sending a normal email, which will probably involve clicking <u>Send Now</u> or <u>Send Mail</u>

3 Send your file as an attachment from your regular email program when you have filled in all of the address details.

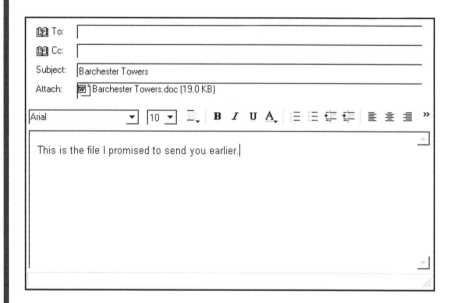

BROWSING THE WEB WITH WORD 2000

As well as sending email within from Word 2000, you can also browse the web from within it. You can search for additional information or clip art, images and new fonts, for instance. The main tool for browsing the web through Word is the <u>Web</u> toolbar, which is accessible through the <u>VIEW/TOOLBARS/WEB</u> entry in the main menu bar. This toolbar will provide you with all the standard icons and facilities of a web browser, plus allow you to stay within Word.

Back/next arrows. Navigate forward and backward between visited web pages.

The Go button allows you to enter the web address you want to visit.

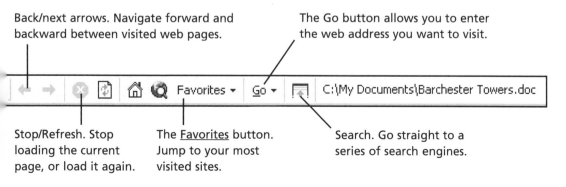

Stop/Refresh. Stop loading the current page, or load it again.

The <u>Favorites</u> button. Jump to your most visited sites.

Search. Go straight to a series of search engines.

CREATING WEB PAGES

Word 2000 contains a powerful tool for quickly creating effective web sites – the Web Page Wizard. You can also use ready-made templates or just build a page from scratch. Whichever option you choose, Word will help you to create a professional-looking site in a short space of time, using text, graphics and even a variety of multimedia elements.

The Web Page Wizard is just one of Word 2000's ways to help you get things done quickly and effectively.

To begin using the Web Page Wizard, create a new document by selecting FILE/NEW in the main menu, then Web Page

Wizard in the Web Pages tab. The Web Page Wizard will ask you a series of questions, and guide you through building a site, offering you many design, style and location options along the way. The Wizard helps you to create a site very quickly and is probably best used if you are in a hurry, or if you really do not want to partake in the site-building process. The options that you get from the Web Wizard are very straightforward and we won't go into them in detail here – it really is a case of just following the instructions and answering a few questions. Once you have experimented with the Web Page Wizard, you may find that you want to start building your own sites with a higher degree of control. Here, we will concentrate on how to go about building your own web site from a blank document and how to tailor it to your precise needs.

USING A TEMPLATE

It is easy to bypass the Web Page Wizard if you want. A good way is to simply select one of the web templates from the FILE/OPEN menu. If you like, you can use an existing Word 2000 document. All you have to do is save it as an HTML document (the format that web pages are saved in) by clicking on FILE/SAVE AS and then select HTML in the File Type box. You can even batch save a whole folder of documents – you may want to convert a series of documents and then combine them into a new web site – by choosing the item FILE/NEW and clicking on the Other Documents tab. Pick the Batch Conversion Wizard and follow the instructions given.

BUILDING A SITE FROM SCRATCH

You can also create your web site from scratch. Start a new document by clicking on the New Document icon and switch to Web Layout view (VIEW/WEB LAYOUT in the main menu, or by clicking on the view icons at the bottom of your working window). You can put together a web site as you would any other document. You can import pictures and write text, and Word will lay them out for you and build your site as you work. You can also add plenty of elements to make your pages interesting, such as graphics, text, tables, sounds and even movies. Just carry on as if you were working on a standard Word document, and let the program handle the HTML. There are a few features that you won't be able to use though, because they are not supported by web browsers. These are line, paragraph and character spacing; margins; and some font effects – such as embossed, shadowed and engraved. These will not be available to you in <u>Web View</u>.

While you are in <u>Web View</u> mode, notice how the text wraps in the window – the margin adjusts to the window's size so you don't lose any text – when you resize it. This is because your work window acts temporaily as a web browser (the program that you use to look at web sites) does. This becomes slightly more complicated with placement of pictures, so it is a good idea to place your graphics in tables if you can. This allows you to set your table to be aligned anywhere on your document, with pictures on one side and text on the other. The tables will still appear as you set them up when they are viewed in any browser.

BACKGROUNDS

If you would like to add a background to your web page, choose <u>FORMAT/BACKGROUND</u> to add some colour or a picture to your page. Images that are imported as backgrounds will automatically be tiled, so a seamless texture is going to look better than a normal picture. Other features you may want to add to your pages include horizontal bars. Click <u>FORMAT/BORDERS AND SHADING</u> in the main menu bar and then <u>Horizontal Line</u> to get the following dialog box:

Use the <u>Horizontal Line</u> dialog box to select line styles to include in your web pages.

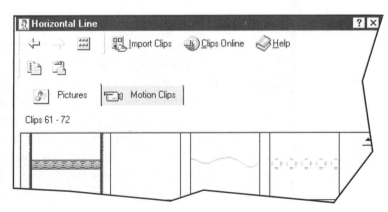

MULTIMEDIA

If you would like to add sounds and video to your page, use Web Tools toolbar, accessed from the VIEW/TOOLBARS/ WEB TOOLS entry in the main menu bar. Adding multimedia elements into your web pages is simply a matter of placing the cursor in the right place, clicking a button and browsing for the file you wish to insert into your page. First use the Web Tools toolbar to select the type of media that you want to insert.

The Web Tools toolbar contains all the elements you need to liven up your web page.

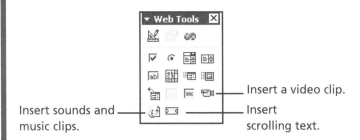

Insert sounds and music clips.

Insert a video clip.

Insert scrolling text.

Then browse through your files until you find the one you require. Word will only offer you files that it can recognize, so you don't have to worry whether a file will work in your web page or not. Adding sound is easy:

Add sound effects and music by clicking on the Sound icon.

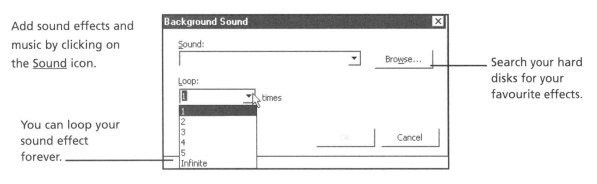

Search your hard disks for your favourite effects.

You can loop your sound effect forever.

The sound will start playing as soon as the page is open in the browser.

SIZE MATTERS

Keep your files small. The bigger the file size a multimedia element or image is, the longer it will take to download it from the internet and view it. The longer your visitor has to wait, the less likely they are to come back to your site.

Selecting a movie clip is just as easy. Click on the <u>Movie Clip</u> button in the <u>Web Tools</u> toolbar. The two main file format standards are AVI and QuickTime, so Word will normally just offer you examples of these to place in your pages.

Select which movie clip to show, and tell Word where it is on your hard drive. You can loop movie clips as you could sound effects (see the previous page).

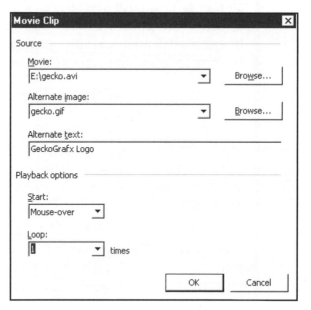

START
Movie clips are notoriously large files. To avoid forcing your visitors to wait for the clip to load when the page opens, you can let them select to view it if they pass their mouse over the clip (<u>Mouse-over</u> option from the dropdown menu), or when they click on it (<u>Mouse-down</u> option).

ALTERNATE IMAGE
Use this to display an alternate image for people whose browsers can't display video. If you don't, there will be a blank in the page where your video clip should be.

ALTERNATE TEXT
The information you type here will appear in the box where your clip is supposed to go, as a description. People who have not selected to have videos in their browsers will be able to read this. Choose some text that relates to the clip inserted.

SCROLLING TEXT

Scrolling text is easy to set up and easy to update.

Call up the Scrolling Text dialog box by using the Web Tools tool bar. Set colours and loops as well as the speed of the text that you use.

Control how the text is going to behave:
Scroll, Slide or Alternate, using the dropdown menu.

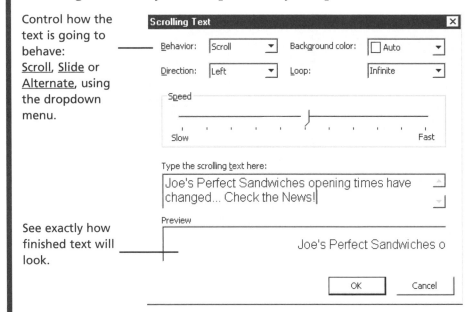

See exactly how finished text will look.

HYPERLINKS

A hyperlink is a very important part of all web sites. We discussed hyperlinks between documents earlier in this chapter and saw that they linked different documents or parts of documents to one another. Used on the internet, a hyperlink connects part of your page, say an image or an underlined piece of text (so people can tell that it's a hyperlink), to another part of your web site or to another web site. A hyperlink picture is often a button, making it obvious that clicking on the link will take the user elsewhere. Text that is hyperlinked will usually be underlined and is often in a different colour from the text surrounding it. When the user moves their mouse over

HTML

HTML stands for HyperText Markup Language. It is a way to code documents so that web browsers can read them. Word 2000 can save any document in HTML format when you select FILE /SAVE AS and choose Web Page: html in the file type box.

a hyperlink the pointer will change from an arrow to a hand icon. Placing a hyperlink is easy. First, you should select the text or the image that you want to use as a hyperlink and choose <u>Hyperlink</u> from the <u>INSERT</u> entry in the main menu, or type <u>Ctrl+K</u>. The <u>Hyperlink</u> option is also available with a right-click in a selected text or image.

1 The <u>Insert Hyperlink</u> dialog box, where you will find everything you need to create and manage hyperlinks.

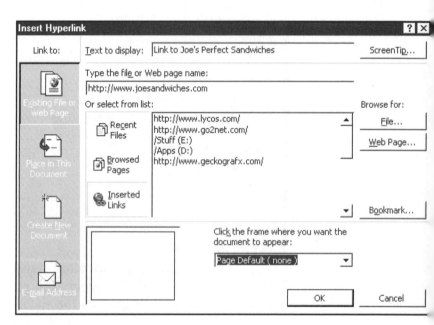

In the <u>Insert Hyperlink</u> dialog box, you can choose exactly where your link will go to – in other words, the page that will appear when people click on that link in your site. In the <u>Link to</u> box, select from the options, each of which has its own details for you to specify. You can link to files that you already have on the internet, to someone else's web pages, or to a point in the document you are working on, or you can create a new document that you will be linking to. Using the <u>Browse for</u> buttons will bring up options that allow you to simply click and select files or web pages to specify them as hyperlinks. You can just input the address of the file you want to link to, or choose to link to a page that you have visited recently. A history of these is displayed in the central box. You can even search the bookmarks you have in your document by clicking on the <u>Bookmark...</u> button. You can specify the frame in which your hyperlinked page will appear if you are using a frameset (for more on frames see page 158). A very useful interactive feature is the ability to have an email address as a hyperlink. When you have set this up and the link is clicked, it causes your visitor's browser to open an emailer and send email to the

Type in the text to be displayed in your email's subject line.

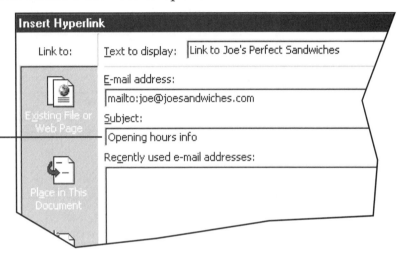

address you specify. If you select <u>E-mail address</u> in the <u>Link to</u> box of the <u>Insert Hyperlink</u> dialog box, you will be given an email address to fill in, with a <u>mailto:</u> prefix. The <u>mailto:</u> prefix tells browsers to send an email to this address. The address that you type after <u>mailto:</u> is the one you would like your mail sent to. In the <u>Subject</u> box, fill in the subject as you want it to appear in the email. When you have input the correct information, click <u>OK</u>, and Word will automatically insert all your hyperlinks correctly for you.

FINISHING YOUR SITE
Once your site is complete, verify that everything is set up properly by selecting <u>FILE/WEB PAGE PREVIEW</u>. This will give you an idea of how your page is going to behave in a real web browser, so you can see exactly what your viewers will see. If you have any problems, you can go back to Word to try and correct them. Some of your pictures may be too big, for example, or some text may not appear as you expected it to.

FRAMES

Frames are commonly used on the internet to organize navigation, as in a site with a menu bar down one side and text and images across the rest of the page. When the menu is clicked on, it stays where it is and the rest of the page changes. Each of the elements (the menu and the text) is in a separate frame. Frames are like mini web pages inside full web pages.

This is a basic frameset: the main page is divided into two separate frames.

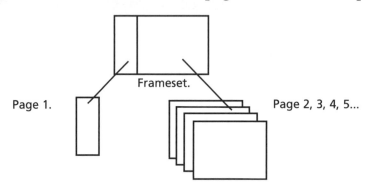

Page 1.   Frameset.   Page 2, 3, 4, 5...

To create the page in the example above, you would need at least four separate elements: the frameset (one page), page 1, and pages 2 and 3 (and so on). When you accessed the frameset, you would click on the hyperlink in page 1 which would change the page on the right hand side of it from page 2 to page 3. Page 1 would not change. Frames are very useful for creating sites that have a consistant style to them.

PUBLISHING YOUR PAGES OVER THE WWW

To publish your page on the world wide web, start the <u>Web Publishing Wizard</u> by clicking on your Windows <u>Start</u> button and selecting <u>PROGRAMS/ACCESSORIES/INTERNET TOOLS/WEB PUBLISHING WIZARD</u>. If this option is not installed, you should contact your network manager or web administrator. The wizard will ask you to name your web site and then to enter the address of your internet server. If you do not possess this information, ask your Network Administrator or Internet Service Provider. When you have this address, connect to the Internet. The wizard will automatically access your web server and upload your pages for you.

CUSTOMIZE WORD

9

When you have used Word for a few sessions, created some documents and printed them out, you will probably find a couple of things that aren't perfect for you – the wrong key stroke for a certain command, or even no key shortcut for your favourite function. Word is fully customizable, so you can modify your menus, add buttons to your toolbar and even get rid of functions you don't want. If there is a feature you can't do without, make it readily available from a convenient right button click.

AUTOMATIC FUNCTIONS

Word 2000 makes things easier for you by providing you with lots of automatic functions. It will automatically correct your spelling mistakes, finish your typing for you, save files… It can be oppressive sometimes, and these functions are not always to the point. Do not despair though, for you can turn everything off, or at least modify the way it works.

1 Everything is controlled via the all-powerful Options dialog box, accessed through TOOLS/OPTIONS.

Options

Track Changes | User Information | Compatibility | File Locations
View | General | Edit | Print | Save | Spelling & Grammar

Show
- ☑ Highlight
- ☐ Bookmarks
- ☑ Status bar
- ☐ ScreenTips
- ☑ Animated text
- ☑ Horizontal scroll bar
- ☑ Vertical scroll bar
- ☐ Picture placeholders
- ☐ Field codes

Field shading:
Never ▼

Formatting marks
- ☐ Tab characters
- ☐ Spaces
- ☐ Paragraph marks
- ☐ Hidden text
- ☐ Optional hyphens
- ☐ All

Print and Web Layout options
- ☑ Drawings
- ☐ Object anchors
- ☐ Text boundaries
- ☑ Vertical ruler (Print view only)

Outline and Normal options
- ☐ Wrap to window
- ☐ Draft font

Style area width:
0 cm

This is a big dialog box, but don't be intimidated – you have already seen several of its tabs in other parts of the book.

The default tab is the <u>View</u> tab. This is where you control what you do and do not wish to see in your document. Depending on the task at hand, you can choose to view characters that are usually hidden, such as spaces, paragraph marks and tab characters. Turn them on or off by ticking or clearing the relevant boxes.

KEEPING TRACK

One of the tabs available to you is the <u>Track Changes</u> tab. You can change the way inserted and deleted text is displayed for instance. The deleted text will not just disappear, but will stay there for you to compare to the new version. The same process can be applied to formatting too.

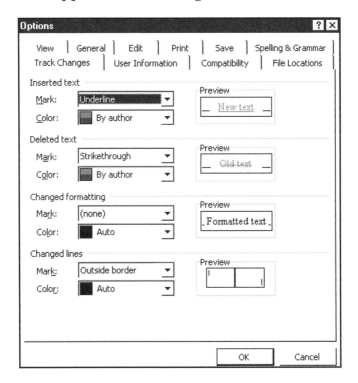

Leaf through the tabs to learn more about the way you can change Word 2000's behaviour to suit your needs. They are laid out by general sections, clear and self-explanatory. Remember that online help is always at your fingertips.

AUTOTEXT

When Word thinks it knows what you're going to type, it will offer to complete the word or phrase for you with a tool tip in front of your cursor – such as when it suggests "Special Delivery" if you type "special". You may find this irritating after a while. To be fair, the majority of users find this option intrusive, annoying or just plain unhelpful. You can turn if off if this is the case.

Uncheck this box to disable AutoText tips.

Select the entry from this list.

Check out what this particular entry is about before making up your mind.

If you selected some text prior to bringing up this dialog box, it will be there for you to add to the list.

Insert the entry into your text or delete it if you don't think you will ever use it.

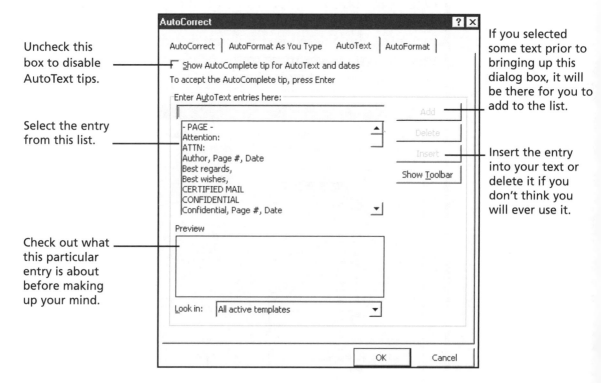

The AutoText tab of the AutoCorrect dialog box is where you take control over Word's automatic typing functions. It is accessed by clicking on INSERT/AUTOTEXT/AUTOTEXT in the main menu bar. Clear the Show AutoComplete Tip for AutoText and Dates box to stop receiving those aggravating AutoComplete messages. Selecting an AutoText option from the list lets you insert specific phrases or changing information – such as the date, time and page number – into your text at the cursor by selecting it and clicking Add.

The <u>AutoText</u> toolbar, brought up by selecting <u>VIEW/TOOLBARS/ AUTOTEXT</u>.

Go to the AutoCorrect dialog box.

This button will provide you with a list of entries to paste into your text where your cursor is.

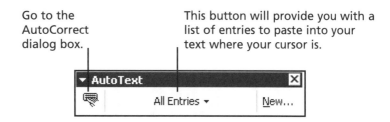

Add your own <u>AutoText</u> entries by selecting a phrase and clicking on the <u>New</u> button on your <u>AutoText toolbar</u>. A dialog box will ask you for a name for your new entry which will afterwards be available in the drop down list, in a category named after the current style.

AUTOCORRECT

One feature that is popular with Word users is <u>AutoCorrect</u>. Word 2000 will correct the most common mistakes typists make, such as "eth" and "nad". But you can also add your own common mistakes to the list. To do so, open the <u>AutoCorrect</u> dialog box via <u>TOOLS/ AUTOCORRECT</u> in the main menu. First, check the list of common mistakes. If there is a mistake in here you feel sure you are not going to make, you can opt to delete it. When adding a common error, be careful about the way you type the element to be replaced and the one that is going to replace it. It is often advisable to add a character space before and after the word, so that the change applies to a whole word rather than to a group of letters in a correctly spelled word, for security. For instance, if you type "golves" all the time, don't set "olves" to change to "loves" because then "wolves" will be changed into "wloves". In the same vein, if you added a space before or after an element to be replaced, mirror this in the element that is replacing it, or you may end up with words stuck together.

Fine tune your <u>AutoCorrect</u> options with these tick boxes.

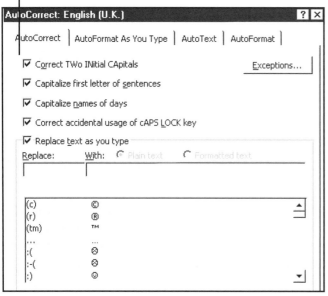

Here is a list of common typing mistakes. Fill in your own commonly-misspelled examples in the <u>Replace</u> and <u>Replace with</u> boxes.

CUSTOMIZING YOUR TOOLBARS

Word has hundreds of buttons, icons, toolbars and things. It has stuff you will probably never use... If you were to view all the toolbars available, the result would look something like this:

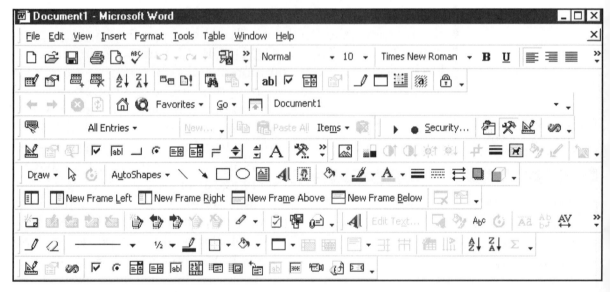

It is really daunting to see all the icons available at the same time.

GETTING ORGANIZED WITH TOOLBARS

There are simple ways to customize your work environment. You already know that you can resize the toolbars and make them float around your screen. You can also place toolbars at the bottom of your work window, including the main menu if you so wish. Word will remember where the toolbars are positioned every time you start it up.

At the far right end of your toolbars is a small down arrow entitled <u>Add or Remove Buttons</u>. Passing your mouse over this button will open a floating popup menu with all the buttons for that particular toolbar in it. Click to the left of the icon you need and the icon will be added to the toolbar itself. If you are not satisfied with your changes, click <u>Reset Toolbar</u>. Underneath that is another button, that will bring up the <u>Customize</u> dialog box, shown below.

Control and organize your toolbars with the help of the <u>Customize</u> dialog.

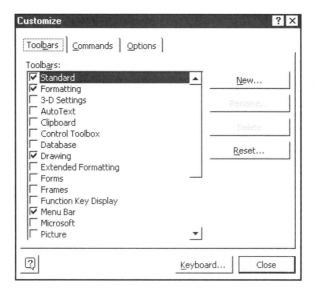

The first thing to do is to open the <u>Toolbars</u> tab. From this, activate a toolbar you wish to modify by selecting its tick-box. The chosen toolbar will appear in your work window. You can create an entirely new, empty toolbar by clicking on the <u>New</u> button.

If you choose to add a new toolbar, you'll see the <u>New Toolbar</u> dialog box:

Select what template this toolbar will be available to. The default value is the Normal template.

Give your new toolbar a name. You will be able to rename it later (or even delete it altogether).

Once the name and template are entered, a small, empty toolbar will be created next to the <u>Customize</u> dialog box. You can make this toolbar into a useful resource easily though, by moving or copying other icons to it, or by adding commands that don't normally have an icon short-cut of their own.

The <u>Commands</u> tab in the <u>Customize</u> box lets you add/remove commands from toolbars and menus.

Select a menu from this list to see what commands it contains.

If you are not sure what a command does, click this button to get a description of it.

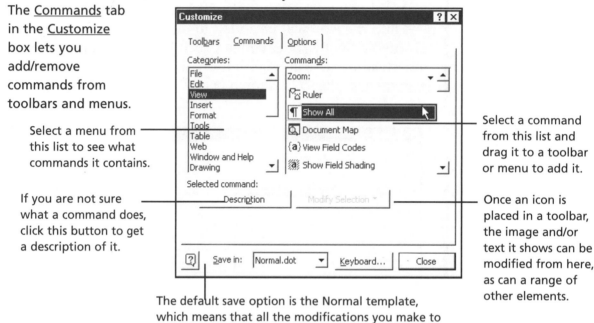

Select a command from this list and drag it to a toolbar or menu to add it.

Once an icon is placed in a toolbar, the image and/or text it shows can be modified from here, as can a range of other elements.

The default save option is the Normal template, which means that all the modifications you make to your toolbars will be available every time you start a new blank document.

While in customize mode – as soon as you have the <u>Customize</u> dialog box active – you can also click and drag icons already displayed in any toolbar to another position, even in other toolbars if you want. You can add, move or remove menus and menu items in exactly the same way. You will see your mouse pointer change into a fat vertical bar as soon as you reach a place in a toolbar where you can relocate your menu or icon.

EDIT EVERYTHING

Try using the <u>Edit Button Image</u> and <u>Change Button Image</u> entries via the <u>Modify Selection</u> button to modify the extra icons you add, giving them a unique personal look.

You can control certain general elements of the behaviour of your toolbars and menus with the Options tab of the Customize dialog box.

If you prefer to see all menu items at once and not just the ones you commonly use, uncheck this box.

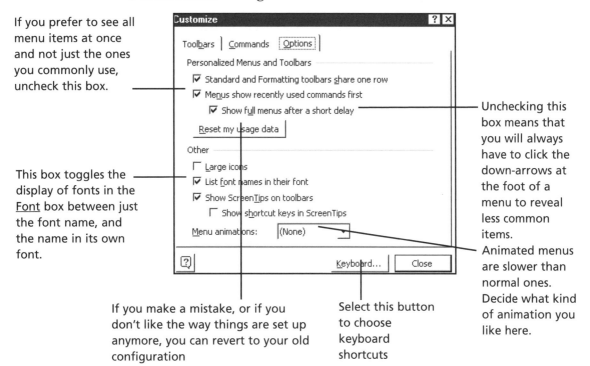

Unchecking this box means that you will always have to click the down-arrows at the foot of a menu to reveal less common items.

This box toggles the display of fonts in the Font box between just the font name, and the name in its own font.

Animated menus are slower than normal ones. Decide what kind of animation you like here.

If you make a mistake, or if you don't like the way things are set up anymore, you can revert to your old configuration

Select this button to choose keyboard shortcuts

ASSIGNING A KEY TO A COMMAND

Each menu item, icon or button can have its own unique keyboard shortcut that you set up via the Customize Keyboard dialog box. As with toolbar customization, you first select a category and then a command via the relevant tabs as described earlier. Type the combination of keys you wish to assign to this command. If this combination is already used, the old current command will be displayed. As the new shortcut key supersedes the current one, be careful not to overwrite a shortcut that is used all the time, such as Ctrl+S. If you are satisfied with your shortcut key, click the Assign button. If not, either click the Reset All button or highlight the shortcut in the Current Keys box and hit Remove. The shortcut key combination will be deleted.

MACROS

Macros are automated tasks that you define yourself. They look like little programs within Word 2000 and are extremely useful, especially when you assign them to a shortcut key. While getting the best from macros requires a thorough knowledge of Microsoft's Visual Basic programming language, there are plenty of valuable uses you can put macros to without any programming, as they will record a sequence of key-presses and commands for you.

You can assign a macro to a shortcut key or to a toolbar (click here, choose the toolbar and hit <u>Close</u>). For now, assign it to the keyboard. ⎯⎯⎯⎯

Select which template you want the macro to be available in. If you choose "Normal", it will be available for all future new documents.

Enter a description of your macro. By default, the user name and the date will be displayed. Highlight this and type over.

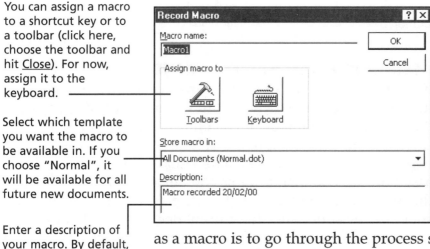

Macros will let you record any common sequence of key and mouse presses as an easily repeatable function, such as returning to the start of a document and typing your address. The easiest way to learn how to record a series of commands as a macro is to go through the process step by step. Select <u>TOOLS/MACROS/RECORD NEW MACRO</u>. First of all, you will need to enter a name for the new macro. It is best to use something relevant to the macro involved. The name must start with a letter and contain no spaces.

Once you have chosen a name and template for the macro to be identified by, you need to assign a keyboard shortcut for it. This will be by far the easiest way to access the macro, so make sure that it is a combination that you can remember fairly easily, ideally one that has some sort of relevance to the macro you are going to record. When you have chosen a keystroke for it, click Close to start recording the new macro.

1 The Customize Keyboard toolbar is the same for Macros as for custom buttons and menu items.

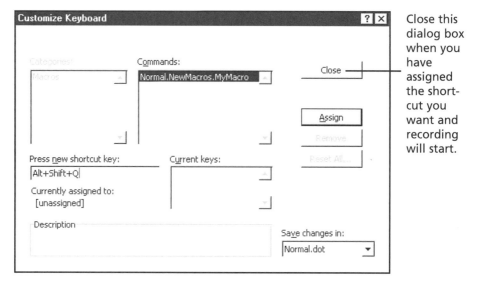

Close this dialog box when you have assigned the short-cut you want and recording will start.

As soon as macro recording begins, a small floating toolbar containing a stop and pause button – just like a tape player – will appear on the screen, and the mouse pointer will change into a tape cassette icon. From that point on, every action you take – keystrokes and typing, through menu or icon commands, entering info into dialogs, inserting objects, file saving or anything else – will be recorded until you hit Stop. As soon as the recording is stopped, the macro is completed and can be activated. Pressing the keyboard shortcut will appear, to Word, identical to carrying out the recorded actions. Most recorded macros like this are typing shortcuts, such as a label or address.

1 Once you have started recording a macro, you can close the Macro Recorder window if it is in the way. Word 2000's menus will change <u>TOOLS/MACROS/ RECORD MACRO</u> into <u>STOP RECORDING</u>.

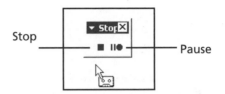

Stop — Pause

Use the <u>Pause</u> button if you need to perform an action you don't want recorded, such as browsing the help files for instance. If you forget to pause, the action will be recorded. Click on the <u>Pause</u> button again to continue recording.

CREATING MACROS FROM SCRATCH

Another way to create a macro is to program it from scratch. Clicking on <u>TOOLS/MACROS/MACROS</u> or typing <u>Alt+F8</u>. will bring up the <u>Macro</u> toolbar from which you can create a new macro as well as editing the ones you have already created. Select a macro in the list (or type a name for your new one) and then hit the relevant button. <u>Run</u> will insert the selected macro where your cursor is. <u>Edit</u> will simply edit the macro while <u>Step Into</u> will run it and stop at each command line. <u>Create</u> will present you with a blank project. This is very advanced, so don't try it unless you know what you are doing.

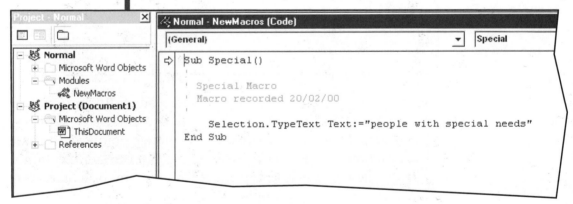

This is the <u>Visual Basic for Applications Development Environment</u> window that will open when you click either on the <u>Create</u>, <u>Edit</u> or <u>Step Into</u> buttons. Macros are built with Microsoft Visual Basic and can be extremely complicated, although the Macro above is fairly straightforward.

SECURITY

Security, unfortunately, is an extremely important issue. Hackers and virus writers across the world have a particular fondness for Word macros. A whole range of viruses are designed to attack Word documents, and your computer, if you do not check it for macro viruses. To avoid getting a system infection, always run a virus detection program in the background, especially if you download Word documents from the Internet. A second step is to set the security level of your system by choosing TOOLS/MACROS/SECURITY. You have various levels of virus protection from within Word 2000. The higher the level of protection you select, the more secure your work is. You don't have to abandon macros altogether though. If you are certain that a document from a particular person cannot possibly be infected, you can enable macros from that source. Additionally, in the Trusted Sources tab, you will have a list of sources that have been digitally signed and that are designated as guaranteed safe.

Security [?] [X]

Security Level | Trusted Sources |

○ High. Only signed macros from trusted sources will be allowed to run. Unsigned macros are automatically disabled.

○ Medium. You can choose whether or not to run potentially unsafe macros.

○ Low (not recommended). You are not protected from potentially unsafe macros. Use this setting only if you have virus scanning software installed, or you are sure all documents you open are safe.

No virus scanner installed.

[OK]   [Cancel]

This is an invitation to disaster. Always have a virus checker running in the background, for your own sake as well as that of the collaborators who are going to work with your documents.

SECURITY OVER THE INTERNET   [_] [□] [X]

If you are working with files over the Internet that are infected with a macro virus and your virus checker keeps on sounding the alarm, this is because, although you can delete the virus from your local file, the source file on your Internet server is still corrupted. To remedy to that, download the correct document, disinfect it, and then copy it across to replace the infected document on the server – or better still, contact your Network Manager.

LITTLE-USED FUNCTIONS

There are several seldom-used functions in Word 2000 that can make your Word Processing easier. The ones covered here – Word Count, Table of Contents and Index – can all be used to surprisingly good effect once you are confident in your abilities using the less complex functions of Word.

WORD COUNT

This is very useful function that will do a whole lot more than just count the words in your document. Particularly handy for novelists and writers of all types, it has its own entry in the main menu under <u>TOOLS/WORD COUNT</u>.

The Word Count dialog box doesn't just summarize how many words you have typed so far but shows the statistics for your whole document.

At the end of a spell check or a grammar check, you can display a readability score by activating the <u>Show Readability Statistics</u> box in the <u>Spelling and Grammar</u> tab of the

TOOLS/OPTIONS menu. Not only will you get a word count, but you will also get an idea of how readable your document is, according to two tests – the Flesch Reading Ease score and the Flesch-Kincaid Grade Level score. The average score for the first test is around 70, and the score should be around 7 or 8 for the second test – the higher the score the more complex the text. Note that a spell check or a grammar check will take longer to process with this option turned on.

Readability Statistics

Counts	
Words	356
Characters	1612
Paragraphs	8
Sentences	11

Averages	
Sentences per Paragraph	1.8
Words per Sentence	30.2
Characters per Word	4.4

Readability	
Passive Sentences	18%
Flesch Reading Ease	55.6
Flesch-Kincaid Grade Level	12.0

OK

TABLE OF CONTENTS

The Index and Tables dialog lets you create a table of contents. This function lets you generate a list of the contents of your document for easy reference use.

1 Call up the Index and Tables dialog box from the INSERT/INDEX AND TABLES menu. The table of contents that is created will be based on the Styles you chose while setting up your document. Different heading styles will correspond to different Table of Contents levels.

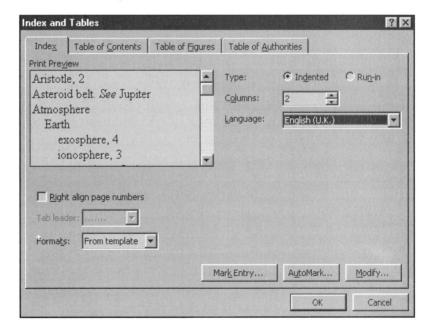

Index and Tables

Index | Table of Contents | Table of Figures | Table of Authorities

Print Preview

Aristotle, 2
Asteroid belt. *See* Jupiter
Atmosphere
 Earth
  exosphere, 4
  ionosphere, 3

Type: ◉ Indented ◯ Run-in
Columns: 2
Language: English (U.K.)

☐ Right align page numbers
Tab leader: ....
Formats: From template

Mark Entry... | AutoMark... | Modify...

OK | Cancel

2 Each heading in your document will map to a corresponding level in the table of contents that you create, unless you define a different order by using the Options dialog.

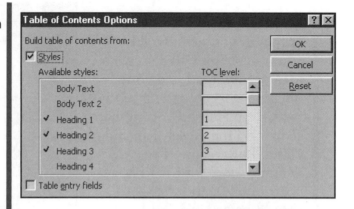

AUTOFORMATTING

If you did not remember to use Heading Styles in your document,you can still add a table of contents by using the AutoFormat option (FORMAT/AUTOFORMAT). Word will go through your document, automatically assigning heading styles where it sees fit. It will not always be right, so the most secure option is to select AutoFormat and review each change instead of simply Autoformat now. Word will search through your document, noting styles for the various parts of the text. When it has finished, it will present you with a Review window from where you can view all the changes it would like to make. Modify these as necessary before accepting them. You might need to have a few goes before you get exactly what you want, but it is worth experimenting. With headings present, you will be able to create a table of contents.

INDEXING

An index can be an invaluable addition to a complex document. Word can help you with this, and it is just a question of telling it which entries you want to be included in the index and then choosing the style. First of all, you need to mark the words that you want in the index. The number of words that you choose to appear in your index will depend on the number of words in your document – as a general rule a short document should have a short index. You should mark key words, concepts, people and places that are mentioned. When the Mark Index Entry dialog box pops up it stays open, so when you have marked your entry you can switch back to your document and mark more entries straight away. Select a word or phrase and switch to the Mark Index Entry box, which will enter the selection into the Main Entry box. If you need a subentry for the item, type it in the Subentry box. For example if the entry was "Banana" you may want it to appear under a "Fruit" subentry. Use the Options to select the way the information is going to be displayed – as a Cross-Reference (Banana, *See* Fruit), as a simple single-page entry (Banana 34), or as a Page Range (Banana 34–35). When you have selected all your options, click Mark to add the word as an index entry. Clicking Mark All will mark all the occurrence of the selected text as an index entry. When you are done, place your cursor at the end of your document (or wherever you want the index to appear) and select the Index and Tables dialog box once more. Clicking OK will tell Word to generate an index and place it at your current cursor position.

1 Add words to your index before you create it. Select the word or phrase and use Shift+Alt+X. This brings up the Mark Index Entry dialog box.

Mark Index Entry

Index
Main entry:
Subentry:

Options
Cross-reference: *See*
Current page
Page range
Bookmark:

Page number format
Bold
Italic

This dialog box stays open so that you can mark multiple index entries.

Mark   Mark All   Cancel

An index should be created when everything else in your document is finished. If you create an index and then change the contents of the document – even adding a few phrases can be enough – the index will no longer be accurate and you'll have to generate another one.

SHOWING AND HIDING SPECIAL CHARACTERS

All the entries in an index are marked by a piece of hidden text, which means that the <u>Index Field</u> – something that Word uses to remember that a certain word will be in the index – will not be seen unless you want to see it. Word uses other hidden characters too, so that you can, if necessary, see what is going on behind the scenes in your document. Other examples include the spaces between words, paragraph breaks, page breaks and section breaks.

Word automatically shows you all of the hidden fields, including the index fields – as an {XE "your text"} line after your entry – when you click on <u>Show/Hide Special Characters</u>. To hide these fields again, click off the <u>Show/Hide Special Characters</u> icon.

In this document you can see word spaces, tabs, paragraph breaks and an index field.

CHAPTER·I¶
¶
Who·will·be·the·New·Bishop?¶
¶
→   IN·the·latter·days·of·July·in·the·year·185—,·a·most·important·ques–tion·was·for·ten·days·hourly·asked·in·the·cathedral·city·of·Barchester{·XE·"Barchester":·\t·"See·Towns":·}·and·answered·every·hour·in·various·ways·——·Who·was·to·be·the·new·Bishop?¶
→   The·death·of·old·Dr·Grantly,·who·had·for·many·years·filled·that·chair·with·meek·authority,·took·place·exactly·as·the·ministry·of·Lord·——·was·going·to·give·place·to·that·of·Lord.·The·illness·of·the·good·old·man·was·long·and·lingering,·and·it·became·at·last·a·matter·of·intense·interest·to·those·concerned·whether·the·new·appointment·should·be·made·by·a·conservative·or·liberal·government.¶
→   It·was·pretty·well·understood·that·the·out-going·premier·had·made·his·selection,·and·that·if·the·question·rested·with·him,·the·mitre·would·descend·on·the·head·of·Archdeacon·Grantly,·the·old·bishop's·son.·The·archdeacon·had·long·managed·the·affairs·of·the·diocese;·and·for·some·months·previous·to·the·demise·of·his·father,¶

DESIGN BASICS

10

Preparing your data is only one part of creating a good document. You must take into consideration whom your document is destined to be read by, and check whether you have chosen the right format and the right style for the task. There are simple and effective rules to designing successful documents involving use of colours, indentations, images and fonts. Follow these guidelines and, with a bit of imagination, you will come up with a letter or a report that will hit straight to the point and at the same time look agreeable.

DESIGNING DOCUMENTS

The most important consideration for a perfect document is clarity. Your document must be easy to read, its various sections easily accessible and relevant to the themes developed. For an example of good design in practice, have a look at one or more of Word 2000's pre-prepared templates. You can also feel free to base your own designs upon a corresponding Word template to help with style.

Use one of Word's many pre-designed templates for your new document.

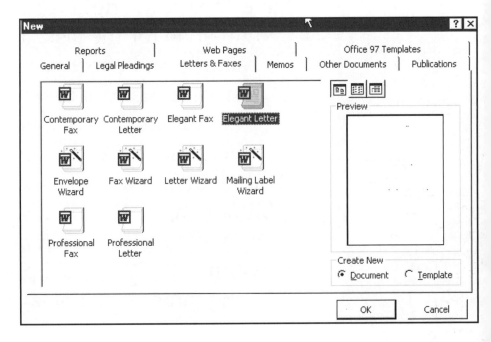

AUDIENCE

The design of a document has to change dramatically depending on the purpose it is for and the people who are going to read it. Preparing a formal financial report involves an entirely different set of design assumptions to designing a leaflet to announce an approaching birthday party. In general, the more serious a document is intended to be, the more restraint you will need to show in its design, and this is the assumption that we will be working with in the bulk of this chapter. To make sure important information is conveyed with maximum impact, if you use pictures, they need to be subtle and unobtrusive, and not distract the reader's attention from the key points of your document.

Clarity often goes with understatement. A single graph or picture will have much more impact than a dozen will. Even if you need a lot of pictures, they may get to be too big, or contain elements that are not relevant. This is not a reason to discard an image though – use the Crop button on the Pictures toolbar to get rid of anything you don't need, and thereby focus the reader's attention. If you need to resize a picture, make sure you hold down the Shift key and use the corner handles as you do so, otherwise the picture will lose its aspect ratio and will become squashed or elongated.

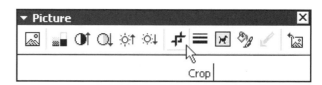

1 Select your image, click Crop, and resize it, holding Shift to keep the same shape.

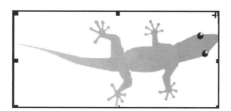

CAPTIONING

Most images can be improved through the use of a caption. The Word 2000 <u>AutoCaption</u> utility is available, but it can only really categorize pictures – Spreadsheet 1, Spreadsheet 2, etc. A far better answer is to manually write a short sentence for each picture explaining its origins, purpose or key message. This will help make sure that the message the picture is illustrating is conveyed as effectively as possible. You can also further distinguish a picture with a subtle border to separate the body text from the illustration.

OVER-DESIGNING

A common mistake when designing a document is to go too far with headings, fonts and effects all over the place. There are plenty of fonts available for free on the internet, but most of them are very specific and will simply not go with certain styles of document. Try to restrict yourself to just the fonts you need for impact. Two or three different fonts will add variety, whereas 20 will confuse readers. Just because a font looks good, it doesn't necessarily follow that it'll work in your document.

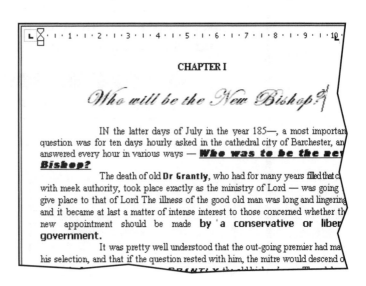

This document has been seriously overdone. The number of fonts used make it almost unreadable.

FONT FUNDAMENTALS

For the main text of a document, known as the body text, it is usually a good idea to use a standard font, one that Word installs on every machine, such as Times New Roman. Your reader will be used to it. Some handwritten fonts look good, but if you use them as the body text, the reader will soon be struggling – which you do not want. Use fonts, headings and subheadings to break up your work, arranging it in small, manageable sections and, once a style has been chosen, be consistent. A blank line can also do wonders occasionally. Use Print Preview mode to get a feel for the look of your document. If you have one paragraph running for a whole page or more, you need to edit it down into a number of smaller paragraphs to help preserve legibility. If you overwhelm the reader, you will only cause irritation and fail to get your message across.

1 Check your paragraph lengths with Print Preview mode, and make sure you aren't making them too long.

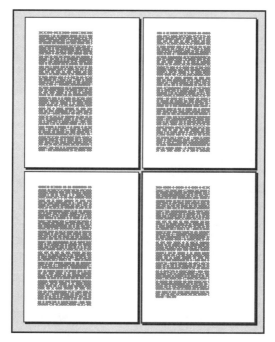

You can see at a glance that the paragraph above is far too big. It looks like a huge block of text that runs forever. Remember that people usually read a paragraph in one go, pause to take in what they've just read, and then continue.

COLUMNS

If you use columns, beware of the "three words per line" syndrome. It makes reading very difficult. Instead, reduce the number of columns, justify the text and insert a horizontal break from time to time. Make sure that the columns are evenly spaced and that the text is nicely and evenly distributed between them without too much distraction.

In the above example, the columns are wide enough but the first line indent is far too big, and looks incongruous. In the second and third columns, the right edge is too ragged as well.

COLOUR IT UP

Colours are another way to enhance the readability of a document by drawing attention to critical areas. However, overuse of colouring and shading or the close proximity of nastily clashing colours will go a long way to distract and alienate your reader, leaving your work mostly wasted. Choose colours that go well together and do not provoke bad reactions, and use them sparingly. For most purposes, pastel colours will usually do the job better than garishly crude neon tones and eye-bending cross-hatches.

DROP CAPS AND WATERMARKS

There are more ways to add a subtle touch to your text. One common answer is to use drop caps or a watermark.

> I n the latter days of July in the year 185—, a most important question was for ten days hourly asked in the c
> Barchester, and answered every hour in various ways — Who was to be the new Bishop?
> The death of old Dr Grantly, who had for many years filled that chair with meek authority, took place exactl
> of Lord — was going to give place to that of Lord The illness of the good old man was long and lingering, and it
> matter of intense interest to those concerned whether the new appointment should be made by a conservative or l
> government.

A drop cap is the term for a paragraph in which the first letter is considerably larger than the others – three lines deep is standard – with the remaining text fitting around it. First select the text you want to add a drop cap to (generally just the first paragraph of a chapter or section) and then select FORMAT/DROP CAP. You can choose the type of drop cap you want from the dialogue box. To remove a drop cap, click on the paragraph containing it and click on <u>None</u> in the <u>Drop Cap</u> dialog box.

A watermark, finally, is an image that will appear in the background of a printed document. A watermark must not interfere with the text and is therefore light, nearly transparent. Watermarks are inserted in a Header or Footer block. Choose <u>VIEW/HEADERS AND FOOTERS</u> from the main menu bar and then <u>INSERT/PICTURE</u> to place one. You may have to modify the size of your image to place it exactly.

I n the latter days of July in the year 185—, a most important question was for ten days hourly asked in the cathedral city of Barchester, and answered every hour in various ways — Who was to be the new Bishop?
The death of old Dr Grantly, who had for many years filled that chair with meek authority, took place exactly as the ministry of Lord — was going to give place to that of Lord The illness of the good old man was long and lingering, and it became at last a matter of intense interest to those concerned whether the new appointment should be made by a conservative or liberal government.
It was pretty well understood that the out-going premier had made his selection, and that if the question rested with him, the mitre would descend on the head of Archdeacon Grantly, the old bishop's son. The archdeacon had long managed the affairs of the diocese; and for some months previous to the demise of his father,
rumour had confidently assigned to him the reversion of his father's honours.
Bishop Grantly died as he had lived, peaceably, slowly, without pain and without excitement. The breath ebbed from him almost imperceptibly, and for a month before his death, it was a question whether he were alive or dead.
trying time was this for the archdeacon, for whom was designed the reversion of his father's see by those who then had the giving away of episcopal thrones. I would not be understood to say that the prime minister had in so many words promised the bishoptic to Dr Grantly. He was too discreet a man for that. There is a proverb with reference to the killing of cats, and those who know anything either of high or low government places, will be well aware that a promise may be made without positive words, and that an expectant may be put into the highest state of encouragement, though the great man on whose breath he hangs may have done no more than whisper that "Mr So-and-so is certainly a rising man".

GLOSSARY

This book has been written using a minimum of technical terms. Nevertheless, you may have come across a few here and there: after all, it is difficult to talk about an engine without using words like "carburettor" and "crankshaft". In case you had any problems with a particular term, here is a list you will find handy.

AUTOSHAPE
Part of Word's drawing facilities, these are graphic objects (simple or complex), ranging from geometrical figures to banners.

CELL
Single element in a table that can be filled with data, text, images or formulas.

CROP
To crop is to take away part of an image by using the handles without re-sizing it.

DATABASE
A collection of individual records containing rows of information. Use a database to create a mail merge for instance.

DIALOG BOX
A window displayed by Word so that you can configure an operation or when Word needs more information from you.

DOCUMENT MAP

A hierarchical display of the main points in your document, based on the headings you used. Ideal to quickly browse and rearrange the structure of your work.

DRAG

To left-click on an item and move it around while keeping the button pressed. When you release the button, the item stays where the mouse is.

FIELD

Part of a record containing information when you create a database. Word also use fields as pieces of codes inserted in your text that contain special information such as the date or time that is updateable.

FILE

Any kind of document as far as your computer is concerned. Files can be anything, from Word documents and templates to dictionaries and programs…

FONT

A set of characters having the same style. Fonts are useful to assign a particular mood to a document or a paragraph.

FOOTER

Information or text that is added at the bottom margin of your printed document. The footer usually contains a page number.

FORMATTING

Changing the look of your document by changing the attributes of a character, a paragraph or a whole page.

FORMULA

Series of logical operators used to perform calculations in a table.

FRAME

A window within a window in a web page. Usually used for a menu or a table of contents.

GUTTER

The space left aside for binding on two facing pages.

HEADER

Information or text that is added at the top margin of your printe document.

HEADING

Powerful feature in Word that will itemize your document. Idea to create document maps and tables of contents.

HYPERLINK

A jump from one item to another (be it a bookmark, a file, anoth page you created or a page someone else created somewhere on the internet). Hyperlinks are usually displayed as a line of underlined text, but they can be assigned to a graphic too.

ICON

A small graphic that symbolizes an operation. Click on it to laur the operation it depicts.

INDENT

Used to move a whole paragraph quickly by a tab stop space.

INVISIBLE CHARACTERS

Set of characters you do not usually need to see in a document, such as spaces, paragraph markers or tab characters. Use the Option menu to see them.

LEADER

A line of dots or dashes added between two tab stops in a table.

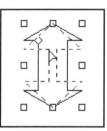

MACRO
A series of instructions, usually recorded step by step, that automates a task. Macros can be assigned to a keyboard shortcut or a toolbar.

RESIZING HANDLES
Squares around a graphic or a text box that enable you to resize it when you click and drag.

RIGHT-CLICK
To use the right button on your mouse to access special dropdown menus.

SHORTCUT
A combination of keystrokes that will speed up an access to a dialog box or an operation.

SPECIAL CHARACTERS
Symbols and international characters such as accented letters.

TEXTURES
A seamless graphic you can add to a web page background or to the front face of a piece of WordArt.

TOOLBAR
A series of icons specific to a certain range of operations (formatting operation, drawing operations…), aligned on a grey bar. Toolbars can be dragged around the screen or locked together at the top or the bottom of your work window.

WORDART
A range of preset, fully configurable text effects.

WEB RESOURCES

The web is the place to find information and resources to add that extra bite to your documents or web pages. There are literally thousands of sites to browse for that perfect clip art or animation. Here are a few sites to start your search.

MICROSOFT

The first place to look for additional information is of course the Microsoft homepage, found at http://www.microsoft.com This site is huge, but there is a very efficient search facility throughout and help, as for all Microsoft products, is available at the click of a button. It helps to know exactly what you need before going there though.

Microsoft is also the software company that produces your operating system, Windows. Windows has a feature called Windows update, accessible from the Start button. Let Windows check its configuration and update itself so that you are running the latest version.

SEARCH ENGINES

A search engine is a web site that will search all the web pages currently available for a particular topic. Try typing "free fonts" or "free pictures" and you get a list of all the relevant sites dealing with free pictures and free fonts. The best known search engine is probably Yahoo at http://www.yahoo.com. Try http://www.altavista.com, http://www.lycos.com or http://www.go2net.com.

CLIP ART

In one of the search engines listed in the previous page, type "free clipart". You will see that there are lots of sites dedicated to providing you with free stuff. Most of these sites are private and all of them are crammed with freebies, usually arranged by easy to browse categories.
http://www.clipartconnection.com is one of them, along with http://www.artclipart.com. All these sites have links to other freebies sites, so don't hesitate to have a look around for that special piece of clip art. Clip art is usually copyright free, but do make sure before you use it.

FONTS

The same process applies to fonts. From outrageous, out of this world fonts to proper handwritten ones, they are all to be grabbed from somewhere on the Web.
http://www.fontfree.com is a good start. All the fonts are listed by category and you usually get a preview of them online. Note that Microsoft also has a collection of fonts at your disposal at
http://www.microsoft.com/typography/fontpack.

WEB TOOLS

http://www.thefreesite.com is a good place to go for free stuff. You will find animated images, seamless backgrounds, JAVA scripts, counters, horizontal bars, free graphic and font programs... and if you don't find it here, there are scores of links to other useful sites. Most of the information is easy to access and to integrate into your web pages.

COVER DISKS

Another source of inspiration and free tools are computer magazines' cover disks. They often feature free clip arts and free fonts for your PC. Check out the computer section at your local newsagent from time to time.

INDEX